EMERGING FROM TURBULENCE

EMERGING FROM TURBULENCE

Boeing and Stories of the American Workplace Today

Leon Grunberg and Sarah Moore

ROWMAN & LITTLEFIELD
Lanham • Boulder • New York • London

Published by Rowman & Littlefield
A wholly owned subsidiary of
The Rowman & Littlefield Publishing Group, Inc.
4501 Forbes Boulevard, Suite 200, Lanham, Maryland 20706
www.rowman.com

Unit A, Whitacre Mews, 26-34 Stannary Street, London SE11 4AB,
United Kingdom

British Library Cataloguing in Publication Information Available

Library of Congress Cataloging-in-Publication Data
Grunberg, Leon.
Emerging from turbulence : Boeing and stories of the American workplace today / Leon Grunberg
and Sarah Moore.
pages cm
Includes bibliographical references and index.
ISBN 978-1-4422-4854-0 (cloth : alk. paper) — ISBN 978-1-4422-4855-7 (electronic) 1. Boeing
Company. 2. Aircraft industry—United States—Management. 3. Aircraft industry—United
States—Employees. I. Moore, Sarah, 1965– II. Title.
HD9711.U63B63294 2016
338.7'629130973—dc23
2015022612

∞ ™ The paper used in this publication meets the minimum requirements of
American National Standard for Information Sciences Permanence of Paper
for Printed Library Materials, ANSI/NISO Z39.48-1992.

Printed in the United States of America

CONTENTS

ACKNOWLEDGMENTS

Our research on Boeing began some twenty years ago when we approached the company with the request that it let us study how the workforce would respond to corporate change. We had no idea that the changes would be so deep, ongoing, and widespread or that we would be fortunate to study Boeing for such a long period of time during which it was radically transformed. It still produced amazing airplanes, but how and where the airplanes were designed, manufactured, and assembled changed significantly, along with its company culture and identity. Focusing on the first decade of the transformation, we documented with longitudinal, quantitative data, collected from thousands of employees, why and how Boeing changed and with what consequences for the employees. Our findings can be found in many academic papers and in *Turbulence: Boeing and the State of American Workers and Managers* (2010). In this new book, we want the aftermath of that decade of change to be told in the words of the employees, not only because they have value in themselves but also because we believe the stories will resonate with many other workers and managers employed across a wide swath of the American economy.

Returning to ask employees who participated in our research for so many years to once again take the time to answer our questions depended heavily on their generosity. We are profoundly grateful that so many of them have trusted us enough and thought our endeavor sufficiently worthwhile to help us again. We are also delighted that new, and mostly younger, Boeing employees found the project interesting and worth contributing to. Although their identities are disguised and we cannot thank them by name, we owe the thousands of employees who helped us a great debt. We hope we have done justice to their stories.

We are also grateful to the National Institute of Alcohol Abuse and Alcoholism of the National Institutes of Health for funding the first phase of our study and to The Boeing Company for giving us access to dozens of managers and thousands of workers who participated in the research. Local 751 of the International Association of Machinists and Aerospace Workers (IAM) and the Society of Professional Engineering Employees in Aerospace (SPEEA) also gave us access to their membership so that we could conduct the most recent phase of the study. The cooperation of the unions has been invaluable. We thank Stan Sorscher and Ed Lutgen for their support of the project and help in facilitating our connection with the unions.

A very special thanks also goes to Ed Greenberg, who helped launch and nurture this project from its inception and who was an inspiring collaborator on all phases of the study and on nearly everything we've written on the Boeing story. Only distance and time have prevented him from collaborating fully on this book. His perceptive comments on the manuscript have greatly improved the final outcome. We also wish to thank Pat Sikora, another outstanding colleague who was part of our research team during earlier phases of the project.

Interviewing so many individuals required a team of dedicated assistants. We were fortunate that Kristen Ching, Mackenzie Fuentes, and Sarah Leonard displayed the sensitivity and empathy to gain the cooperation and trust of those they interviewed. We struck gold with Emily Sterling. She conducted many of the interviews and developed remarkable rapport with employees of all ages. Her open, down-to-earth personality and her exceptional probing skills elicited some very revealing interviews. She is truly a gifted interviewer.

In addition to the University of Puget Sound for financial and sabbatical support and Reggie Tison for excellent administrative assistance, we are grateful to the many friends, relatives, and colleagues who read the entire manuscript and provided insightful suggestions. These include David Smith, Cooper Sherry, Michael and Suzanne Moore, Elizabeth Hirschl, Dawn Rodin, and Sarah Anne. Emma Grunberg's editorial suggestions were exceptionally astute and clarified and sharpened our writing. Of course, we are responsible for any remaining errors. For his contributions during initial phases of the 2013 survey construction and background work, we wish to thank colleague Alan Krause. Finally, over the many years of this project, we have also benefited from the support and encouragement of our colleague and friend Sunil Kukreja and from our spouses, Sonia Grunberg and Cooper Sherry.

I

BOEING'S TRANSFORMATION AND AMERICA'S NEW SOCIAL CONTRACT

When I say I changed the culture of Boeing, that was the intent, so it's run like a business rather than a great engineering firm. It is a great engineering firm, but people invest in a company because they want to make money.

—Harry Stonecipher, 2004, former CEO of The Boeing Company, reflecting on the late 1990s

They have changed my attitude to be "why should I care" and to look out for myself as management won't. Also, Boeing is no longer a premium company to work for. If I can find something—anything— somewhere else, I'm gone. They got no loyalty to me, why should I have any to them?

—Technical employee, twenty-three years at Boeing, interviewed in 2006

"This is no longer your father's company!" That was the pointed proclamation a top executive reportedly made to Boeing employees shortly after the company merged with McDonnell Douglas in 1997. Newly installed company leaders were intent on boosting financial performance by shaking the workforce out of its cozy, laid-back ways. The message to employees was that they should let go of the past and come to terms with the new corporate reality. A new governing ethos, some say imported from McDonnell Douglas, would focus on minimizing risk and improving shareholder returns. The changes would also shake the working lives of employees and profoundly affect their relationship with their company.[1]

It might seem unremarkable, or at least uncontroversial, that a giant corporation would foster a workplace culture that placed profits first. But for many employees, the changes that accompanied Boeing's merger with McDonnell Douglas threatened the very identity of the company: a much loved and highly valued family culture that had driven their engagement in their work and commitment to Boeing. As described in the *Seattle Times*, "Under the family culture, beginning with Bill Boeing in 1916, bold aviators focused on grand visions of building ever better, faster, bigger aircraft. Management of the company was anchored in loyalty and promoting through the ranks."[2] Indeed, so-called Heritage Boeing employees were extremely proud of building innovative, safe, quality products, such as the 707 and 747, airplanes that set the global standard in commercial aviation when launched. Executives told their employees—and the employees believed—that they were number one in the world, as indeed they were until Airbus gradually ate into Boeing's market share and achieved parity in deliveries in the early 2000s. The company was known for providing excellent pay and benefits, arguably among the best in the country for comparable jobs, and this was viewed by employees as evidence that the company valued their skills and dedication to the organization. Top company leaders truly knew the products: first and foremost they were engineers with a passion for aviation, and employees trusted them to make competent decisions.

Boeing also offered lifelong employment and the promise of a meaningful career. Opportunities for growth and promotion were endless, and despite the cyclical nature of the industry and the accompanying mass layoffs, one could work at Boeing for life, as could members of one's family. It was commonplace for one's parents, grandparents, children, siblings, aunts, and uncles to work for the company. And even though the company employed thousands of people in the Puget Sound region of Washington State, many of them spoke warmly and even intimately of the "Boeing family." Commented a longtime engineer about his workmates, "I've been to weddings. I've been to funerals and Christmas parties. I've got friends I've done dog sitting for. Our families will get together." Employees felt strong emotional ties to their coworkers and supervisors and even to the airplanes they built and the very buildings where they worked.[3]

But following the merger, Boeing's new leadership—responding to Wall Street pressure for higher returns and steeped in what veteran Boeing employees regarded as McDonnell Douglas's cutthroat culture[4] —actively eroded the qualities of Heritage Boeing that had generated such loyalty and enthusiasm. In his now infamous 1998 statement, Harry Stonecipher (Boeing president and chief operations officer and former McDonnell Douglas CEO) cautioned employees to "quit behaving like a family and become more like a team. If you don't perform, you don't stay on the team."[5] Living through the turbulent time of change that followed was very difficult for veteran employees. For many, morale plummeted, commitment to the organization weakened, trust in top management's competence and ethics reached an all-time low, and employees' physical, mental, and emotional health suffered. "I've changed my vision of who Boeing is," wrote a female office worker in 2006. "It's a big corporation that will use my services when it needs them and flush me out when it doesn't. While I am here, I work my eight hours, but my loyalty is to my family, my friends, and my community in that order."

This fundamentally transformed company, however, is no longer new: company leaders have made clear that they do not intend to resurrect the Heritage Boeing model. For well over fifteen years now, Boeing's strong emphasis on shareholder value, increased attention to costs, and greater concern with profit has been made evident in dozens of decisions, some of which have been less than successful. For example, excessive outsourcing of the 787 Dreamliner[6] and the opening of a second 787 assembly line in South Carolina, done to control costs and spread risk, led to massive problems, a 3.5-year delay, and a serious blow to company pride. Boeing has taken a more forceful attitude to unions, using the location of new programs as leverage in negotiations, and within a few years none of the workforce will receive guaranteed pensions. Indeed, the dust has settled on the larger issue of company identity. Boeing truly is no longer "your father's company." Whatever the costs, prioritizing shareholder value is here to stay.

THE NEW SOCIAL CONTRACT

The Boeing story is a dramatic example of corporate transformation, but it is not an isolated one. We have been struck by how often those who read our work or hear us speak about the changes at Boeing tell us that their organizations have gone through similar transformations. Employees in health care and education and at corporate giants like 3M and IBM, for example, have also experienced the cost cutting, the leaner production processes, the expanded outsourcing, the loss of benefits, and the narrowed focus on financial metrics that have roiled Boeing.[7] Researchers, such as sociologist Beth Rubin, have documented these trends, writing about the broad-scale industrial restructuring sweeping the nation in the 1990s and identifying additional corporate changes such as the prevalence of mergers and the weakening of union power via tactics such as relocation to right-to-work states, sending work overseas, and implementing technological innovations—all changes Boeing undertook.

As this process unfolded across corporate America, the postwar employment "social contract" between workers and management was radically redefined. Although it had been an implicit contract, American employees had widely understood that hard work and good performance would be rewarded with a living wage, good benefits, job security, and even meaningful work. Companies, too, would benefit from this arrangement in the form of a stable, well-trained workforce that generated profits. This understanding, however, has been replaced by a new ethos: the chase for short-term shareholder returns. Under this new arrangement, top management is purported to care less about securing the long-term loyalty and psychological commitment of its workforce. Some observers of this shift have predicted the increased fragility or even the demise of the American Dream.[8]

There have been many books and articles written by scholars and commentators who have, on behalf of American workers and families, lamented the deleterious effects these recent trends have had on employees' income, health, work, and family lives.[9] There is also no shortage of "how to change your organization" books or laudatory stories of "heroic" leaders rescuing or "saving" their companies against stiff odds. Battling resistance from powerful interest groups or ossified bureaucratic inertia, intrepid executives become superstars by successfully transforming their companies.[10]

This book is different. We have sought to chronicle a dramatic corporate transformation through the stories of those most directly affected: the employees themselves. Admittedly, the millions of "ordinary employees" who work in corporate America rarely have starring roles in these unfolding dramas of change, but they are the ones who endure the insecurities and uncertainties when restructuring or downsizing or outsourcing decisions are made. A full understanding of the consequences of corporate change is not complete without their voices.

We report the stories in the employees' own words.[11] From over eighty in-depth interviews derived from our extensive research that studied company changes from 1996 to the present day, we have selected thirty-six individual narratives for this book. The narratives are arranged into three groups: retirees who spent most of their work lives at the company; long-serving but still-employed workers who witnessed the transformation firsthand and have had to adjust to and cope with the new Boeing; and newly hired employees with no direct familiarity with Heritage Boeing. The interviews probed many facets of employees' work lives and experiences but sought primarily to understand the long-term impacts of such a profound company transformation. By comparing the views of these three groups, we are better able to see the complex and nuanced picture of how employees find meaning at work and how they connect emotionally to the company today. We can also begin to detect whether such change portends significant shifts in employee attitudes and expectations, with potential costs and benefits for employees and companies both at Boeing and beyond.

Focusing on employee stories illuminates, perhaps even more clearly than quantitative survey data, the powerful but not-easily-measured impact of Boeing's new postmerger business paradigm. Companies don't just make products or generate profits. They also create cultures and engage emotions. How does one put a dollar value on "working together," "going the extra mile" for one's company, or feeling the deep emotional identification with a company that is rooted in the local community and nurtures a family ethos? And will new employees be as critical as some old-timers are about the loss of "family," prioritizing shareholder value, and excessive outsourcing, or will they accept the changes as the "new normal" and perhaps see them as opening up new opportunities? What does it matter that one's retirement is recognized or that one receives a signed card from his or her workmates after a loved one has passed away? Of what financial benefit are company-sponsored volunteer activities? How will companies be able to develop a committed workforce when many of the mechanisms to engage employees have been weakened or abandoned? Indeed, do large companies care as much as they used to about the emotional ties that bind employees to their companies? Intangible benefits, by their nature, are difficult to price and measure. Some executives may therefore assume that they are not terribly important for company profits—at least not in the short term. This collection of stories suggests a different conclusion. Indeed, it is another form of evidence that something important is lost, perhaps not in quarterly-earnings reports but in the lives of workers and in the meaning and sense of well-being that work can provide.

Moreover, whether they are on the factory floor or at their desks, employees often have invaluable knowledge of workplace problems and insightful suggestions as to their solution. We now know that the decision of Boeing's top management to minimize its risk profile by substantially outsourcing the design and production of the 787 was a costly mistake. Even top executives have acknowledged the errors in the plan—3.5 years late and over $25 billion in the hole at this time of writing. But it should also be noted that many employees were skeptical early on of this new business model and warned top executives about the shortsightedness of adopting it.[12] In the following pages, workers raise concerns about several other Boeing policies. They worry about the loss of valuable tribal knowledge, not only due to excessive outsourcing but also when employees retire without careful transmission of expertise to new hires. They regret the rapid rotation of supervisors, preventing teams from building relationships and continuity. They complain that a narrow emphasis on schedule may lead to compromises in quality. Regardless of their validity, these complaints are typically made in a spirit of cooperation and with a genuine desire to improve the company. Indeed, along with the concerns, employees also acknowledge and praise Boeing's focus on safety, its good pay and benefits, and the "amazing" educational and career opportunities it provides.

A FORESHADOWING OF OUR FINDINGS

As one would expect, there are differences in attitudes to the changes at Boeing among the three groups of employees, but one theme is ubiquitous. Regardless of age or tenure, all employees seek to find meaning and purpose in their work lives. They want to make a difference, however small. Whether they helped mentor coworkers, ensured that the planes they built were safe for the millions flying in them every year, or made some creative contribution to the design or manufacture of the product, each had a deep-rooted need to leave a mark. Studs Terkel found the same motivations in his worker interviews over forty years ago.[13] In his eloquent formulation, work is a search for "daily meaning as well as daily bread, for recognition as well as cash, for astonishment as well as torpor; in short for a sort of life . . . to be remembered." Thirty years later, the authors of *Gig: Americans Talk about Their Jobs*, a collection of interviews with some forty individuals in a smorgasbord of jobs, came to a similar conclusion.[14] It is an enduring truth, then, that even as work and organizations are transformed and new generations of workers replace older ones, the need to find some meaning in the years one spends working remains unchanged, a permanent facet of the human drive to give purpose and value to one's life.

In seeking to satisfy this inner drive, Boeing employees had to navigate not only a changed company but also, like millions of employees across America, a vastly different and depressed economic environment as the dismal aftermath of the "great recession" accelerated corporate changes that were already under way. Quite a few of the interviewees accepted these changes as an inevitable by-product of heightened competition and difficult economic circumstances, often noting that despite the cutbacks, Boeing still provided much better pay and benefits than one could find "out there" in the volatile labor market. Younger, newly hired employees in particular seemed to accept the company's single-minded emphasis on profits and shareholder value. "The company's number one goal is profits. I know it sounds cold, but it's true. I don't think there is anything wrong with that," said a twenty-seven-year-old mechanic. Many also embraced the belief that they needed to focus on developing their employability, carving out their own work destinies with an independent, do-it-yourself spirit and confidence. Perhaps it is for this reason that we also heard high levels of pessimism about the future efficacy of labor unions, especially among these younger employees. Older employees, by contrast, were more likely to grudgingly resign themselves to the new business philosophy that underpinned what they saw as ruthless and greedy management practices. Wrote one veteran technical worker, "Boeing no longer wants the best employees. They seem to be content to hire average people and pay them average salaries. I guess that is one way to make airplanes. Boeing used to be about exceptionalism—now it's averagism."

With the emergence of this new social contract, it is not surprising that the types of emotional connections workers feel to their work have also changed. Some employees fail to acknowledge their corporate leaders' explicit disavowal of the "Boeing family" and continue to cling to its memory despite the fact that the new order has been in place for quite some time. Others speak wistfully and powerfully of the loss. And curiously, some still speak of the Boeing family or invoke family-like terms even though they came to the company well after the family-to-team proclamation. For those who have detached emotionally from the company, some find meaning and satisfaction in their day-to-day tasks, while others view work as just a means to a paycheck. For a few, their bitterness toward Boeing's changes has left them completely alienated from the company and from their work.

Most employees we interviewed continued to search for meaning and satisfaction at work, even if they were increasingly motivated by personal achievement rather than company loyalty. As William Whyte remarked in *The Organizational Man*,[15] the older, authoritarian organizations wanted "your sweat," but organizations of the 1950s and 1960s wanted "your soul." Have we returned to a day when employees are expected to offer only their sweat? Do soaring profits mean such a change has not damaged but actually improved company performance? And could there be benefits for employees, as well, when emotional ties to the company are weakened? We return to these questions in the final chapter, but they are addressed implicitly in the employee narratives to which we now turn. Recounting moments of exhilarating pride and deep frustration, these frank stories, told by those most deeply affected, convey Boeing's transformation—and the broad changes to the American workplace reflected by it.

Part I

Retired from Boeing

In this first section, we hear from retirees whose work experiences were predominantly shaped by the Heritage Boeing culture. Although the details of their stories differ a great deal from each other, collectively, they paint a picture of Heritage Boeing where certain motifs are heard repeatedly as they reflect on their work histories. Yes, there is some idealizing as they recount the past, but there is also genuine and enduring affection for the company. As millions of baby boomers across the United States, including thousands of Boeing workers, head for retirement, stories such as these flesh out the historical record of a disappearing era of corporate life. They also establish a point of reference against which workers compare the new, emerging culture and ethos. When retirees or long-serving employees push back against the "new" Boeing, many of them are doing so from what they believed was valuable in the "old" Boeing. Newly hired employees sometimes do this too, but their point of comparison comes to them from stories they hear rather than firsthand experiences. Indeed, understanding the past as told through the stories of retired workers holds great value in understanding the present-day reactions of current employees.

The themes that emerge in the following stories are also echoed in the numerical data we collected in our large, company-wide surveys, reinforcing our belief that these narratives capture representative and salient beliefs and attitudes held by many employees of this generation.

Looking at previous survey data from the age group that had retired by the time we began our interviews in 2011, we find that they were, on the whole, a dedicated cohort. In 1997, they had already accumulated many years of service (on average, twenty), were earning a good income ($63,000), and missed very few days of work (on average, only 1.5 days per year). A sizable number (57 percent) were also confident that labor unions could be "depended upon to protect the American worker."

Surprisingly, and despite the profound changes at the company, many of this group's attitudes toward the company and their jobs didn't change much between 1997 and 2006. Although morale dipped during the middle years of our study, many of our indices of satisfaction, involvement, loyalty, and trust returned to premerger levels. Our data also revealed that employees drew sharp distinctions between how they felt toward The Boeing Company as compared to how they viewed top management. This distinction surfaces repeatedly in the interviews. For example, in 2006—shortly before this cohort's retirement—we see that loyalty, commitment, and pride toward the company are quite high across these ten years, with some 75 percent of employees telling us that they are "proud to work for Boeing" and approximately 60 percent saying that they feel "loyal toward the company." Indeed, one-third of the sample goes so far as to say they would turn down another job with more pay to stay at Boeing. Such powerful connection to the company was expressed by nearly every retiree we interviewed and persisted even in the face of the difficult and painful work events they experienced.

But such warm feelings toward the company did not extend to how they regarded top management: for example, in 2006 only one-third of the respondents indicated that they "believe what top management says," and some 40 percent felt that "top management makes bad decisions." Moreover, a sizable number (40 percent) believed that company leaders neither "care about their well-being" nor "appreciate extra effort" from them; many (45 percent) did not believe that the company leaders created an "atmosphere of trust and respect among employees." These older retired employees were also divided on their views regarding the company's future plans and efforts to bring employees on board. Roughly one-third agreed (and one-third disagreed) with whether Boeing has "created a sense of purpose and meaning shared by most employees," "energized employees around company vision and goals," or "valued different perspectives and ideas on how to conduct business." Indeed, this more negative and divided opinion comes through in the interviews too: some trust Boeing leadership and think the company's future is bright and aptly responsive to today's economic realities. Others, however, feel just as strongly that Boeing is headed in the wrong direction.

Somewhat curiously then, views about management didn't diminish the degree to which these older Boeing employees reported being involved and working hard. While they were not completely defined by their jobs (only some 17 percent endorsed the statement that the "most important things that happen to me involve my work"), a large percentage—roughly 75 percent of the sample—said that they "show up early to get things ready" or "take on extra duties," and approximately 70 percent reported that all things considered, they liked their jobs. Although the reasons for this strong work ethic are many, our survey data point to a strong belief in the social contract among these older employees and retirees. They expected the company to provide a good pension (77 percent), job training (64 percent), long-term job security (56 percent), and quality, affordable health benefits (80 percent). In return, they would remain loyal and dedicated employees.

As we will see in subsequent sections, some of the attitudes we find in this group are mirrored in the views of employees in different age cohorts. Changes in Boeing's culture were not abrupt; the past just doesn't disappear overnight. It lingers in the memory and practices of older employees, even as top management rhetoric heralds a new dawn. Nevertheless, we do find a gradual but noticeable shift in perspective across the generations, as Heritage Boeing employees exit the workforce, younger ones are hired, and the new ethos becomes institutionalized.

2

HERITAGE BOEING

With over one hundred years combined of employment at Boeing, the four employees in this chapter look back with gratitude and satisfaction on their Boeing careers. They are grateful for what Boeing made possible for them and their families. The pay and benefits, as well as the opportunities to try different jobs and to develop close social relationships at work provided by Boeing, easily fulfilled their work expectations. They reciprocated by doing good quality work, taking pride in the product, and working diligently to make a difference. The social contract that characterized management-labor relations in many large post–World War II companies seemed fair and balanced to these employees. The company took good care of them during their working years, and in return they were loyal and dedicated.

They are particularly nostalgic about the old ways of doing things— the hand-drawn designs, the large, open office environments, the care Boeing took with its repeated testing and trials before launching new airplanes, and the supervisors who were intimately familiar with shop floor conditions and how airplanes were made. As these old ways of working were abandoned and replaced by computers and new business practices, some of these older employees became less enamored with Boeing.

What is striking about this group, however, is their relative lack of grievances toward the company or, when they do take issue with management decisions, their capacity to justify company actions and still look back fondly over their careers. For example, even though David

Sutton regrets the abandonment of lessons learned in building the 767 and 777 when Boeing launched the 787 program, he has faith that in the end the plane will be safe and will perform as Boeing executives promised. Similarly, Peter Wall realizes not only that designers would be "absolute dinosaurs" if they still drew on paper but also that computers enhance the accuracy, speed, and sophistication of the design process. Faced with technological and business changes they did not approve of or couldn't keep up with, many retirees have no regrets at all about choosing to retire from Boeing when they did. It was the right time for them. And even as they express nostalgia for "the good old days" and disappointment at some of the directions Boeing took in recent years, they also have no regrets about spending most of their working lives at Boeing. In the words of one retiree, "It was a good ride."

DAVID SUTTON

> I think I'm really lucky because it's very rare in a career that you can pick a product and be associated with it for forty years. I don't feel work is just a paycheck. So that's it; I was lucky to pick Boeing.
> —Engineer, age seventy, forty years at Boeing,
> interviewed in 2012

I couldn't possibly have thought I would be here for forty years. When I think about it, you know, it turns out that I did so many different kinds of jobs. About every two or three years I'd get a different assignment. And they were always increasing in terms of complexity, challenge, money—things that tend to motivate you. My favorite position, one of them, was as a manager in product development, and we'd just done the 757, 767. The Chinese were buying airplanes, but they were also trying to grow their industry and trying to develop airplanes that would fly short distances. They had taken a Russian airplane, it was a World War II airplane, and reverse engineered it. They started flying them without doing the kind of testing we would do, and they started crashing. They had six crashes and they couldn't figure out why. And these were killing people. They were in commercial service and the airplane would come in for a landing, turn upside down and crash, and kill everybody on board. I mean, Lord knows Boeing has crashed airplanes, and we spent a lot of time and effort trying to resimulate that, and understand it, and go back and test it, and figure out what was wrong. Some of the early days on the 707 saw some horrible crashes that were engineering errors that we just didn't foresee. Well, so anyway, they came to Boeing and said, "We need your help."

But Boeing didn't build an airplane that size. So the sales organization came to the engineering organization and said, "Is there anything you guys can do?" So I was asked to put together a program for them. We brought a team of their twenty-five best engineers over to work in Boeing with twenty-five of our engineers and started working on this airplane jointly. We went over to China maybe thirteen times over a period of two years, three years. And we did a wind tunnel test with the airplane at the University of Washington and then took the same model to their wind tunnel test in China. That was a pretty cool project really. None of these guys spoke English. We had to have an interpreter for everything. I got to meet Chinese on a very personal level and found them to be just wonderful. They love what they're doing, they laugh, they have a good time, you know, it was really quite an experience.

The things we did by hand when I first started are done so much more efficiently with computers that it is really staggering. When we started out, we would write a FORTRAN program, and there'd be a woman who would read my equations and type them. Every line was an IBM card and this IBM card would have one statement on it. You'd stack these statements up and put them in a reader. I tell you, it wasn't even five years later each engineer had like four engineering aides, and we'd write out these equations and break them down and the engineering aide would then just take a piece of paper and calculator, like a mechanical calculator—you press buttons and then pull a handle, it wasn't even electric (laughs). Then we got an electric one (laughs). Whoa! Yeah. I mean this is in my lifetime: this isn't in a hundred and fifty years. I mean the changes were just rapid. The things we do now . . . Like to build a wing for a new airplane, we'd do maybe 175, 200 separate wind tunnel tests all over the country; now we do that on a computer. And the airplanes are unbelievably more efficient. They're quieter, burn less fuel, more comfortable, stronger, last longer. I mean, it's been a revolution in terms of the product.

Essentially, you have to figure out how to network. I do remember one time I'd gone to one of my favorite bosses. He was a director when

I worked for him, vice president of customer services, a real responsible job. There must have been fifteen thousand people who reported to him. But I knew him well enough to call him up. It was sort of, "Hi, how you doing?" And he just cut to the quick. He said, "So you must be fifty now" (laughs). I said, "Well, I'm close." He said, "So you're wondering what's going to happen next? What are you interested in? What do you want to do? Do you want to come over and talk to some of the guys over here?" Basically that's why I was calling. He was just so on the mark. He knew! But I hadn't talked to him in probably three, four years. I always felt like I was blessed, or I cultivated, or somehow it happened that I had this contact. So I never felt like I was trapped. Even though it was a big company, you could make those connections. There were just so many talented people at Boeing and so many talented people in executive positions.

Now there were some changes in the organization towards the end of my career that I couldn't do anything about. I didn't think it was the right thing to do. And I really tried to go along with the concept, but I was pretty much the old-school way of doing things. They weren't going to fire me or lay me off because I still was doing what they asked me to do. But, you know, I wasn't going to get any promotions if I wasn't going along with the new organization that was trying to change the way we do business. So that transition was a little uncomfortable. I got to the point where I thought, "Gee, I've done a lot of really cool things and still like what I'm doing. It's been forty years. I've got enough money." So that's why I retired (laughs). After I left, they did make some big changes, changes that I was not in favor of. I'll tell you this, though. Without doing anything in terms of diet or exercise, like fifteen points right off the blood pressure. Just like that. No change, fifteen points lower. Just the stress of getting there, you know, driving at 6:30 a.m. to get there at 7:30. And then e-mail at lunchtime while you're eating your sandwich.

The 787 had a lot of problems. They just didn't have enough time to do the due diligence of test and trial, and test and trial, and make one and see if it worked, and make another and see if it worked any better. Those are real basic, basic things. They just made it, flew it; didn't work. Then they have to turn back the clock a year, and that just blew them out of the water in terms of cost and schedule. And the people that kept saying, like me, "Don't do that to the research," they retired, they left.

They had the experience, they knew, because they'd done it before. They did it on the Triple 7. They did it on the 767. They were there forty years too. But the young minds, they don't want to listen to that kind of stuff. They listen now (laughs). In the end, I'll feel good about the product. I know it'll be safe. I know it'll do what they promised. They'll get there. But that was a big lesson.

I feel really strong about the product. It's the best thing going; I know what goes into making a product like that. And it's staggering. It's five hundred thousand parts that all have to be controlled to twenty thousandths, that all have to perform every day. You know, those airplanes, they fly eighteen, nineteen hours a day, every day for thirty years. And we maintain them—have a whole staff of people that maintain them, a whole staff of people who design them. It's truly the safest way to travel. Just any way you look at it, per mile, per people, whatever. It's an incredible company. I feel very emotional about Boeing, and it's not to say Boeing hasn't done some dumb things, or that they're perfect. [. . .] There are some things that they probably wish they hadn't done, some things they wish we'd done differently. Yeah, that's normal. But, I think that they've been able to be forward enough in their thinking to realize when changes are required and to make them so that they're still in business. It's pretty staggering if you look at Fortune 500 companies, big companies. How many have survived a hundred years?

I think I'm really lucky because it's very rare in a career that you can pick a product and be associated with it for forty years. Our engineering team for a commercial airplane would be five thousand people. But those five thousand people all have to be coordinated, all doing the same thing, working together to build a single product. There's very few industries that you can think of that require that kind of complex design by so many people. I don't feel work is just a paycheck. So that's it; I was lucky to pick Boeing.

MAUDE HENLY

When I fly, I say, "I used to work on these things" or "I used to inspect the wire on these things." It's a very proud badge that I wear.
—Inspector, age sixty-three, twenty-four years at Boeing, interviewed in 2012

I started at Boeing in 1987. I was referred by a friend who said it was a good company—the benefits and the ways they accelerated and advanced people, that the unions kept it fair for everybody. It fascinated me. My first job was building wire bundles; then I moved up to wire installation into shells before I became a quality inspector in the fabrication division. I worked there until 2011 when I retired.

Everyone was very supportive, everyone helped each other. If you didn't know, you could ask someone who had been there awhile. And when you came on the floor you were trained by someone who already knew the job. So I like mentoring. If you messed up, you got a warning, then you got a written, then you were suspended. I managed to go twenty-three years without a warning. I developed a lot of friendships—some were strictly work, and some I know outside work. Going on lunch breaks we all got together and talked. We did potlucks. We celebrated people's birthdays, or baby showers, or whatever. Like a little family. They gave me a retirement party. After being retired for a year, I'm still in contact with some of the people.

When I fly, I say, "I used to work on these things" or "I used to inspect the wire on these things." It's a very proud badge that I wear. [Whenever I travel] I get on the Boeing airplanes or I sometimes have to fly Airbus, and so I compare them. How come I hear this noise? And I'm listening for different noises and things. Before I started working for Boeing it never crossed my mind about the safety of an airplane. After I started working for Boeing, then it started crossing my mind. About the safety of an airplane, you know about, how as an inspector I would find if something was wrong, I would have to put a rejection tag on it. I always think, "What if this got through?" You know, "What if this wiring is bad?" Something could happen, you know. It made me feel good that I could catch something that would keep it from getting on the airplane that might cause an accident and take lives. Being an inspector, I was always very careful about what I inspected. And I double-checked. For a while we were at twelve-hour days, ten-hour days. It took up a lot of my time. That was in the beginning. It was mandatory, and then towards the end, it was more voluntary. At the end I did it because I wanted to. If I started a project on Friday and I wanted to finish, I'd go in because I wanted to finish it and put my stamp on it.

I think what I did made a lot of difference. There were things I would do—a bonding process—if it's just not bonded properly, you know, the lightning strike that happens to an airplane, or building an instrument panel on the pilot's deck—if those things are connected wrong, it's a safety issue. So I think what I did contributed a lot. Even before I got into inspection, building the wire bundles, if you used the wrong-size wire, calls for a twenty gauge and you use a twenty-two, that would cause a short, and something would happen. So I think what I did was very important. Every wire bundle that goes out has your stamp on it. If that wire bundle fails, it can be traced back to the operator. Everyone is very conscious of what they're doing, especially since Boeing now has what they call "self-inspection" in some spots with no one else inspecting their wire bundle. I personally think that people can be a little more relaxed if there's a second set of eyes. You can always find it with someone else helping.

[Whenever I hear of an airplane crash or a plane having a problem,] I'm always hoping that's not a Boeing plane. And then I listen to see what caused it; if it was a pilot's error or a mechanical failure, I wonder if somebody missed something. Or like the plane that went down that had the flashlight on the rear end of the tail section. It caused a short, you know. You can't leave anything. Being an inspector, I think, is quite an important job, 'cause you're the last step to safety before that plane goes out.

When we completed the first 737 and we all got to watch the first test flight that took off from Everett, it was amazing. The unveiling ceremony inside the big hangar, that was nice, but to actually see it fly for the first time—that was unforgettable. I helped do that, I helped. I did that. Yeah. You know, every time they did a rollout, we got little pendants, we got little things to keep for the rollout. I was there for the '87. I felt the trouble we had with the 787 parts that were built in Italy and didn't fit together, the problem might have been eliminated if it was all built here. You can't build something that big over here and over there and expect them to match up.

I think they've got a great future, and they're gonna keep going and become or keep the number one title. Continue improvement on the plans they have, coming up with new ideas. I think it has a lot to do with the way they treat their workers. I mean the jobs are posted. Anyone can apply. I've seen people move up from janitorial all the way up the line in Boeing.

I don't think I would have been as happy doing the work with a different company. It was just a good company to work for. Good benefits, the people, managers, how they interact with the employees. Their values were of honesty, integrity, pride in your work . . . just doing the best you can do. I felt like they treated us fairly. When they merged with McDonnell Douglas, there were a lot of whispers and talk about it, but it didn't affect our work. It did not affect my work. I've been retired for a year, and when I'm sitting at home I get kind of bored. I don't think I want to be doing that no more. I never considered leaving until the time I retired. Actually, if I could, I would go back. I loved my work at Boeing. I've actually put in applications to go back. I had my knee replaced in March of last year, but it wasn't work related so I couldn't get disability for it. And I couldn't go back to work because I was still disabled. So I had to retire so I could still get income. Now that my knees are healed, I'd love to go back to work as an inspector and contribute to the safety of the airplanes again.

PETER WALL

> It's a pleasant feeling about drafting and using your particular penmanship and line style. All that goes away once you use a computer. Your drawings, your design, your text look like everybody else's. The use of the computer design system is extremely frustrating to me.
> —Tool engineer, age sixty-three, twenty-nine years at Boeing,
> interviewed in 2012

We arrived in Seattle on a grey, wet November day, found a hotel, and I reported for work at nine o'clock the next day. They herded all new hires into this big cafeteria, and a very strict lady says, "Don't touch any of those papers until I instruct you to do so." I was seething; I was ready to explode. I had never in my life been treated so impersonally. I was hired as a tool and die quality control inspector. I remember the first night quite clearly. I was used to working at Rolls-Royce, but here I found myself taking measurements with a steel tape. Very unchallenging work. I remember calling my wife at lunchtime and saying I made the most awful mistake. I should never have come here. [But in 1979] I saw an opening for a tool design engineer, and I moved into a salaried job in tool engineering. That was very satisfying, very exciting, because now I was being challenged to be more creative. I was now required to analyze manufacturing procedure and design tooling to help support that. I always had a fondness for design drafting, so it was perfect. I stayed in that line of work for the rest of my time, which was twenty-eight years, alternating between tool design and manufacturing and research design.

Over time my attitude changed; whether that was my fault or Boeing's fault, I don't know. Toward the end of my time, some of the excitement was gone. I pretty much exhausted all of my fresh ideas, and although computer design became a big part of my life and was certainly very fascinating, I didn't get the same satisfaction that I used to get out of working at the drafting table. It was more enjoyable to lay down lines with a pencil; it's not that I'm artistic, it's just that it's a pleasant feeling about drafting and using your particular penmanship and line style. All that goes away once you use a computer. Your drawings, your design, your text look like everybody else's. The use of the computer design system is extremely frustrating to me. I used to describe it as trying to design a piece of equipment without being able to use your hands and doing it over the phone, telling someone else what to do. The computer doesn't have a clue what you are doing. You type in commands of what you want to do. You want to draw a line from point A to point B, you don't just pick up a pencil and do it; you actually communicate with the computer telling it what to do. I found that frustrating.

When I first started in tool engineering in 1979 and saw people working on computer design, I was fascinated. I took an early-morning class and was invited by the leader of the CAD [computer-aided design] group to join his group. I jumped at the opportunity because it was new and different. But later on I found that the type of work in computer design was not very interesting, and so I'd go on loan to different design groups: wing design, body structure. It was so refreshing to go back to using a drafting table that I transferred back and really enjoyed going back to the old way of doing things. But that of course couldn't last; Boeing was moving forward no matter if I wanted to or not. And so, I ended up going back into CAD again, with AutoCAD being the number one CAD system at Boeing. I don't think there was any drafting left at all when I retired. The whole entire 777 airplane—manufacturing, process engineering, design engineering, or tool engineering—it's all interlinked, so you'd be an absolute dinosaur if you chose to draw on a piece of paper. To be honest, I would say it's a tremendous step forwards as far as the accuracy of designs and the transfer of data between you as a tool engineer and the toolmaker. Everything is more sophisticated and more accurate, and you can send a design in seconds to another manufacturer somewhere else in the country or world. So I wouldn't say anything is lost except the good old-fashioned camaraderie in the design office, where you have rows of drafting tables and people scrubbing away with pencils, pencil sharpeners, and erasers, and for me that was the most beautiful time working at Boeing.

We had such good times, having fun, getting on with our jobs. Boeing recently started to emphasize the need for team spirit and team participation. Team spirit and participation was a natural in the old days of open offices with drafting tables and desks and telephones ringing. I remember working in this enormous office which was longer than the street I used to live on and our end of it was the drafting tables, and then you've got all the people who are in planning who wrote the instructions for you to design the tool, and the numerical control programmers. You had this ocean of desks and telephones and people, and it was an environment that was inspiring to me. It was all bustle and busyness, and if there is one thing that I've learned to loathe, it's the cubicle. This wasn't inspired by the popular cartoon; my loathing for it began instantly when I first saw people put in cubicles. I looked at them and said, "What have these people done to deserve this?" I never dreamt that I would end up in one of those things too. I spent maybe ten years in various cubicles and found it the most depressing thing in the whole world. I hate them with a passion. I don't even like saying the word, I usually stumble over it. My coworkers were some of the best friends I've ever had. We always had a great time, always made the best of it. Even in a cubicle you can shadow over the top of somebody, and you know, whatever environment you are in, you always try to make the best of it. People who are in the trenches in the war have fun with each other, so you can't let it destroy you. Without the friendship and camaraderie, I don't think I could function in a workplace.

I don't want to say that I'm a disciplinarian, but one mistake Boeing has made in recent years is, it has become way too relaxed. For example, I was in on the early stages of this newest airplane, the 787, and I had to go and talk to an engineer on the other side of the Everett plant in what they call the twin towers, the two office buildings. When I got there on the Friday, at about 1:30 I think, there was nobody there. I was pacing through all of these wretched cubicles trying to find someone. I thought, "Have they all gone to a big organizational meeting?" I finally found one lonely character sitting there at the computer terminal, and I said, "Is there a meeting that I don't know about?" He said, "No." I said, "Where is everybody?" And he pointed at the windows with the sun shining outside. In the earlier part of my career that would never have happened. Everyone would be accountable, and somebody would want to know where you were. I felt we were really losing a lot of impetus because of being so laid-back and relaxed. These late airplane programs, we get hopelessly behind, and we get delays. Boeing really needs to get people back to a more focused way of doing things. If Boeing could be efficient, it wouldn't need to hire the legions of people it does to get an airplane program finished. They have a philosophy of if you get fifty thousand people, with some luck we will manage to get the output of one thousand people. That's the way they do it. Throw as many bodies as they can, and by the law of averages something should happen.

Work was always important because it was my source of income, but I never wanted to let my Boeing career be the dominating thing in my life. I didn't want to spend all my time working overtime. In the early days I used to do an awful lot of overtime because I felt I was not being supportive if I didn't, and there were times when I would give more than I felt that I should, working Saturdays and even Sundays, feeling that it was my way of supporting the overall effort. But I observed that there were times that I would put myself out to get a project finished only to find that it got held up further down the line and all of your efforts were really in vain. After about fifteen years at Boeing, I said, "No, I'm not going to do that anymore." I started to realize that things weren't as important as people were implying they were. There are lots of young people that are clamoring for overtime and I don't want it and don't need it. I've got things at home to do with two daughters and a wife to think about.

The peak of my Boeing career was during those days in the 1980s in Renton. I used to drive by the Renton plant and say to my wife, "Those were the good old days." I had an extremely supportive lead and supervisor. Both were extraordinary in that they would always say kind words to you in the morning, and it made you feel absolutely wonderful and want to do more and more to please them. One year, my supervisor called me in and handed me an award check combined with the notification that I had been upgraded to a level 5 from a level 4 and said, "Take your wife out to dinner with that." Very nice people, very moving moment. I'm not saying it went drastically downhill after that, but there has never been a time that duplicated those days. Basically managers and supervisors became less personable and personal. Supervisors these days don't want to walk up and down the aisles of cubicles and stop in and ask how it's going. Everything is now on a little tiny screen, whereas in the old days you would be at this big seven-foot-wide, four-foot-tall drafting table. I'm blaming everything on cubicles.

I don't have any regrets about Boeing itself. As I look back now, having retired after twenty-nine years, I kind of regret staying in one place for all those years, but it certainly doesn't have anything to do with Boeing. That was just me, my lack of motivation. I had dreams of traveling around the United States, working here, working there, seeing all the different states. In spite of the fact that at the beginning of my career I loathed it so much I was counting the days until my one-year anniversary was up, because after one year you don't have to reimburse the company for the moving expenses, I ended up spending twenty-nine years. Nobody made me stay there. The only thing I regret is perhaps I should have moved around more and seen more of the country and seen more of the industry, but there are no regrets about staying at Boeing. This sounds silly, but I've always had a tremendous fondness for the British pub. It was a dream of mine and my wife that one day we would find ourselves a little country pub, and we would serve drinks to happy people. We would be polishing the glasses and polishing the brasses. That would have been the realization of a dream for me. But once we got raising a family, all those thoughts sort of drift away.

ANN PULLEY

Engineers and the shop worked together. I don't know how much of that goes on now. Computers can draw, but it still takes a human mind to work out a problem. It can't actually physically look at that part and think, "Maybe this is what went wrong." I hope that Boeing doesn't get so full of themselves with the computers that they hurt themselves.

—Hourly worker, age seventy, seventeen years at Boeing,
interviewed in 2012

I worked in a sewing factory, and one of the young men that worked there was in maintenance. His dad worked for Boeing, and he heard that Boeing was hiring. He was dating my daughter at the time and said, "Go up and put your application in." So I did. And I got called. It was a grade three at that time, an entry-level job. The day I got called and they said I got a job at Boeing, I felt a strange excitement. There were several of us that had worked together in the sewing factory doing piecework that got hired on at Boeing at the same time. I remember us sitting at lunch and talking and saying, "You know, I was still making money when I went to the bathroom" (laughs). Excitement and apprehensive because it's a whole new thing. Boeing is a good place to work. When I first got hired, they were really good to work with. To me the only two reasons you're ever going to get fired from Boeing is poor attendance and stealing. You can make a mistake: they will let you know you made a mistake, but they will help you correct it, and they will help you learn how to not make the mistake again. There's political things that go on. You don't always agree with everything. But it is good money with good benefits.

I was employee of the month once for manufacturing. A supervisor puts you in for it, and then apparently a committee goes through what you've done and looks at your work history and everything. You had a dinner with the management—my direct supervisor, the general, and one other person. And we went to The Keg in Puyallup. You got paid: it wasn't a day that you took on your own time, but you didn't have to go to work that day. You got your picture taken, and they gave you gifts, and they recognized you; they asked that you stood up at the dinner table, explained what you did for the company, how long you'd worked with the company, and then your picture was posted (laughs) in your factory for a while until the next time they took somebody from your factory. I felt special, you know; it was special recognition. I don't know if they do that anymore.

I grew up with four younger brothers, so working with men or boys didn't bother me. Most of the guys that you work with at Boeing are respectful; there's not a lot of dirty jokes or anything like that. Pretty much everybody is professional in what they do. I never felt that my gender made a difference, and I think that most of the women that I worked with felt the way I did. Maybe there was even a little bit of pride that you could do just as good a job as a man could do. And that's one thing with Boeing, is that your gender doesn't enter into your paycheck. You're paid the same as three guys working next to you. You're all making the same amount of money; the only difference would be what stage you are in that grade. In fact, I found men are easier to work with. Women can be a little catty (laughs), and men are pretty much what you see is what you get. If you have a problem with me, I want you to tell me. I find that a lot of women aren't that way. You'll find out if somebody has a problem if the fifth person will tell you about it, where if a guy has a problem with you, he's going to come up and say, "You know, I don't like the way you did this" or "You need to do this this way."

The one girl that I had the closest friendship with, she died of cancer. The things we had planned to do after we were retired didn't happen. It was hard to lose her. We carpooled together. Unless you worked at Boeing, and I suppose it's if you worked anyplace, the only people that understand your work circumstances are the people you work with. Our husbands would get tired of the B word (laughs). They didn't understand. I think carpooling is good if you get somebody that you get along with because you could complain. By the time you get home, that's all gone. You don't take it home and take it to the people that you love and live with. And especially when we worked up at the black hole, because we couldn't tell our families what we did—it was all military secure—we could talk about it to each other on the way home.

You can go to college, but college doesn't teach you how to work with your hands. I think that is one of the biggest problems that Boeing has now. A lot of managers are out of college. They've never done hands-on—I hear that from a lot of people. They have supervisors that don't know how to do the job. They only know how to count numbers. They don't know that it's unreasonable to ask your shop to do 140 parts in a day's time when the capability isn't there. That hurts Boeing. Boeing tried to be a worldwide company. They say that if you can read Boeing blueprints, you can read anybody's blueprints. But I know when they were shipping parts down to Florida that those parts wouldn't fit when they'd come back up to Washington. They'd have to be remanufactured, and if they couldn't be remanufactured, there was a holdup. I'm sure that's what's causing problems with the 787. My son went to

England to show them how to make "cords"—like the ribs that support the wings—but about six months later they sent him back and said we don't want this job. We can't do the job to your specification.

I worked with some really good engineers. The machines I worked on ran on programs that these engineers had to write. If there was a problem with the wing skin, they would come down, and they would talk to us, and they would say, "What do we need to do?" Those engineers and the shop worked together. I don't know how much of that goes on now. Computers can draw, but it still takes a human mind to work out a problem. It can't actually physically look at that part and think, "Maybe this is what went wrong." I hope that Boeing doesn't get so full of themselves with the computers that they hurt themselves that way because I'd like to see my grandson move way up, and I have great-grandchildren, and I would like to see them possibly be able to work for Boeing.

I know that they're trying to cut down on the number of people, even though if you look at a pie chart, wages are a small part of the pie. But it's a part of the pie they can whittle the most. They can't cut down on materials; they can't cut down on their footprint as much as they would like to; so the human element they can control. If the product is still good, then it's something they have to do because they have to compete in the world. I don't think that it's right that they try to compete by going to other countries because I think sometimes they shoot themselves in the foot because there isn't the knowledge. Building airplanes—it's a craft. I think that's why they ran into so many problems with the 787. They made promises, but they didn't have the experienced people. They offloaded too many things.

I've been retired for almost ten years, but it hurts to hear about a Boeing plane crash. It hurts to hear somebody say something bad about a Boeing product, because you know that they're a quality product. I know that the people that I've worked with—they didn't put out a shoddy product. It was all a matter of pride. When you put your love, when you put your stamp down, you said, "I'm proud of that, and it's correct." My mother-in-law worked in Renton installing toilet doors, and every time a plane crashed she always said, "Oh gosh, I hope the toilet door didn't come off" (laughs). So, yeah, there's an emotional attachment. You always want them to be best. I think if you've taken pride in what you've done, you always hold that pride.

3

NO LONGER FAMILY

Like many of the other retirees, the people in this chapter had very fond Boeing memories, especially of their early employment years. They told stories that highlighted exciting, challenging, creative, significant work in which they were able to solve interesting problems, make important work contributions, or lead relevant company-supported volunteer efforts. They talked of meaningful relationships with coworkers that were close and professionally fruitful. Some invoked the word "family" to describe the closeness they felt with their coworkers.

Each, however, was critical—sometimes extremely critical—of the way in which the company's business philosophy changed over time, leading to poor managerial decision making, excessive waste, and unacceptable production outcomes. Their dissatisfaction was connected not so much to the loss of old ways as to the business decisions Boeing made after the merger with McDonnell Douglas. Among the issues employees cited, the company now hired managers who had little knowledge of the product; it lacked critical oversight of outsourced processes and no longer deployed its human resources well; it failed to ensure the transmission of tribal knowledge to the next generation of employees. As Kyle Smith concluded, these changes were so profound that "Boeing has become irrelevant to their own products." This is a strong statement, but one that connotes the depth to which some retirees believed the company's foundational identity was radically altered after the merger.

The impact of this new business strategy was not limited to production-related issues. These employees also remarked—and again with strong emotion—that this transformed ethos was responsible for a new type of company-level disregard for its employees. Mark Lind talked about how the company now possesses "this mentality that all these people are disposable," and he recounted how the company's medical insurance, combined with Boeing's bureaucratic runaround, resisted paying for his cancer treatments. Another described the bold efforts he and his coworkers made to protest many of the changes, only to be ignored and told they were not "team players." And yet another sadly commented several times that the company is no longer a family, something made evident by its failure to recognize workers with much consideration when they retire. Although the degree to which their overarching Boeing-related memories are predominately positive or negative varies widely, they each acknowledge and convey a sadness over the loss of what the company had meant to them during such a long and significant part of their lives.

MARK LIND

> You know, Boeing ate up McDonnell Douglas, but we got a lot of their managers. Some of the dumbest decisions from the workers' standpoint came from that union of those two companies.
>
> —Tech worker, age sixty-two, thirty-five years at Boeing, interviewed in 2012

I was first hired at Boeing in 1974. In my first job we were developing the different communications antennae for the phased array that goes inside the radar on top of the E-3. It looks like a flying saucer on top of the airplane. It was fun—very technical—and some of it was stretching my imagination a lot. After that I went into Commercial—the avionics group for the 777 and 747. We approved the options that defined what their system was going to look like, and then we would ship the whole gamut of engineering releases to get those systems installed on the airplane and test it on the ground, in the factory, on the flight line, and flight-test it. We had to write the certification plans and every piece of engineering from A to Z. You know, it's almost like an ego thing. When people come to you from all over the company because you know more about the system than anybody else, it is very satisfying.

Management is always looking for ways to cut money and typically, if you had an idea that could improve the airplane, you had to show a business case that it would save money even if it was a valuable improvement for the customer. Many times, saving money or staying within some sort of a budget line was more important than having a technically great airplane. It's the people working in the groups in Boeing that make these airplanes as good as they are. I don't believe it is management. I imagine they have a different story, but I never saw any great evidence that management has a whole lot of positive effect on improving the product. They're more concerned about cutting people and cutting budget and keeping salaries down so that we can compete in the international arena.

I had one manager who was saying, "Oh, we can get engineers off the street; we can get them at ten cents on the dollar." I think they abuse their experts—I mean, they know everything about the system, they know what it takes to make the system work, they know what it takes to install it on the airplane, and yet management said, "Oh, you're just a bunch of donkeys. We can get you fresh out of school. We'll fill your position." It's like, you guys are idiots (laughs). It takes a long time—most people would say it takes five years or more—to learn these systems so that you can take on any problem that comes along. It's not something that you just learned last month; you can't just fill those boots right off, fresh off the street. But they had this mentality that all these people are disposable. They didn't really appreciate the engineering talent they had, especially when it came to raises.

I had tremendous relationships at work; it was like a family. It went beyond the professional Boeing thing. A large number of us were really good friends. These guys, I'd like to have them for my brother or my sister, you know. The hardest part about retiring is that the conglomeration of friends dissipates when you leave the company, and they're still back there doing it. They're a fabulous group of people. They would help you when you had a problem, and you'd help them when they had a problem. These systems interreact, they're all interlinked; it is very complex, and it's more than one person can grasp. You have to be of the personality that you can mold into a group of individuals that can help each other and solve the problem and get the airplane delivered.

Here's another thing that really bugged the dickens out of me. When I left, I released my responsibilities to my lead, and when he retired last year, they had no plan for training anybody to take his place. He didn't train anybody to take my place. There's so much knowledge—they call it tribal knowledge—but a lot of times it's not documented. They say, "We want you guys to document your tribal knowledge." But you don't really have the power to do that because you have all these other burdens—airplanes that are flying out every day being delivered. You don't have time to write down everything that you have stuck in your brain; how do you recall all that stuff? Most of the time, you recall the stuff when something triggers it. There's so much hands-on knowledge that is just really, really hard to document.

Retiring in 2009 wasn't my choice. I had to retire a couple years early because I got that nasty C word in 2005. Under the circumstances it was the only thing I could do: I couldn't meet the expectations with the side effects that the cancer gave me. It was supposed to kill me by 2007. I had this big expensive surgery to try to eradicate all the cancer. It's given me an additional five years so far. An oncologist flat told us, "I don't know what else to do for you; I'm sorry; I don't know what else to do." What we did is go on the Internet, and we found out, okay, with this particular strain, who's the best expert in the country or in the world. Anyhow, the crux of it is the insurance company says, "Oh, we won't pay for that; this is out of the Puget Sound network, and what he wants to do to you is considered experimental." We appealed this thing four times. I was also trying to go through the company. I wrote an e-mail to everybody in my management food chain, all the way up to the president of the company. I got responses back from several levels of management in our group, and these people went to bat for me. One manager talked to corporate people in Chicago by videoconference. He told them about my situation. So they said, "Okay, okay, we'll do it, but don't ever bring a problem like this to us again." This is from corporate. I went to DC and was in intensive care for fifty-seven days. He got the cancer out, and I'm still here today.

The problem is that Boeing is self-insured, and the insurance company is contracted by Boeing to administer the medical claims for their workers. The bills actually get paid by Boeing. Boeing would say, "Go talk to the insurance company," and the insurance company would say, "We don't have any control over this; it's up to the company." They were playing this game, back and forth. The bottom line is, if the company tells the insurance company to pay, they have to pay. But they bust their chops trying to figure out a way to not pay for medical benefits. They don't want to provide benefits for their employees, but once they do give them, it's grudgingly. They look for ways to—especially with the retired—cut their benefits, and the retirees don't have any recourse. They have to take it.

You know, Boeing ate up McDonnell Douglas, but we got a lot of their managers. Some of the dumbest decisions from the workers' standpoint came from that union of those two companies. It was almost jeopardizing the integrity of the Boeing Company by absorbing the people who helped drive McDonnell Douglas into the ground. But the Boeing Company is still a pretty robust company. In spite of this economic downturn that we've had for the last four years, their numbers are still pretty good. It's amazing. Maybe they knew that all those managers who didn't know what they were doing, maybe they're actually what keeps the company afloat!

If I was going to do it again, avionics for me is probably the best job at Boeing. I would recommend it to anybody that has electronic experience. It satisfied my technical needs, and the breadth of the responsibilities was really wide, and the authority that you were given was really high. Management didn't know what you were doing as far as how you executed your job, but, you know, you weren't there to satisfy management. You were there to get airplanes operational and working properly, so that scratched my itch.

KYLE SMITH

> What you had at Boeing at the time of the merger was a very collegial, bloated, flaccid management structure. When the McDonnell Douglas guys came in, they just went through them like a knife through butter—just cut their throats, hung them out to dry.
> —Business operations and corporate consultant, age fifty-nine,
> thirty years at Boeing, interviewed in 2012

After I graduated from college I realized that garbage collectors were making twice as much money as I was doing crisis intervention. Their hours and their working conditions were better than mine, and I said,

"Hey, you know, this is a young man's game. I'm going to get into something that society values." So I applied to Boeing. Social services were being cut, the economy was in bad shape, and it was pretty clear to me that social services had very little future. My only alternative would be to get a master's degree, and probably a PhD, and then I'd still be making a third of what I make at Boeing. Plus no health care, no retirement, and I just said long-term, staying in social services is a pretty stupid move. I liked it, but I was unwilling to take the kinds of hits financially.

I'm second-generation Boeing. I worked at Boeing thirty years. My dad worked there for forty. Virtually all of my life I have either worked for Boeing or been part of the family of someone who worked for Boeing. So I care very deeply about the company. But I had absolutely no illusions about the cyclicality of Boeing. That's the downside, the cyclicality. I was very fortunate in that I was never laid off.

I've been in management twice. Didn't like it. Much preferred to do actual work, simply because of the hypocrisy—the fact that all these people were preoccupied with management, and yet they spent most of their time hiding from the workforce. That is literally what they do. They hide. They're afraid of the workforce. For years Boeing has embraced the philosophy that if you can manage a Popsicle stand, you can manage IBM or Boeing, and that it's not necessary to understand the business to manage it. People expect managers to know something about the business, and when they have problems, they want help. That's a legitimate request of management. You know, "I've got a problem, I need your help." But for you to help me, you need to know something about the business. But I met an ever increasing number of these people who simply don't understand the business and, frankly, don't want to be bothered with it. They much prefer the safety of being locked up in their meetings with each other. They don't want to deal with the workforce because the workforce asks them to do things they don't know how to do. And that's embarrassing for anybody.

So you have a workforce that is highly disillusioned, that feels that leadership is out of touch. Management deals with that by hiding and by being increasingly authoritarian. A culture of fear is the only way they have of maintaining control. And it's all done in an environment of encouraging people to tell management what they think, which is absolutely the opposite of what management actually wants them to do. So

you get all of these double messages and double binds that you're putting the workforce in, of saying we want your input but when we get it
you're punished or held back because of it. We want your input, but
when you give it, you're not a team player, because team players only
give us things that make us feel better.

There's also a culture of rotating people around so that oftentimes
you may have very bright people—who may even be inclined to want to
actually learn something about the business that they're managing—but
they're being moved every twelve months. So they never truly learn the
business, but the second, more insidious outcome of that policy is that
they never are held accountable for their bad or good decisions. They
make decisions, the decisions have impacts, the impacts have consequences, but by the time the consequences become apparent, they've
moved on. So they never see the consequences; they're never held
accountable. Consequently, they never learn.

It's a series of serial catastrophes. You see it especially in people who
move up very rapidly. They are moved around so that they can say,
"Yes, I've worked in finance. Yes, I've worked in engineering. Yes, I've
worked in operations. Yes, I've worked in procurement. I've worked in
all of these areas, so I understand the business even though I was only
in them for eight to twelve months." What happens is that they are
aggressively sheltered from the consequences of bad decisions, because
the people who are pulling them up the corporate ladder from the top
don't want them to be embarrassed. So every time it appears that something is going to go south as the result of a bad decision that one of
these bright boys has made, they pull him out, put him somewhere else.
An example is the 757, 767 flight management systems that were being
developed under Condit, which he drove it into the ground. Before it
crashed and burned, they jerked him out and put him in some other
role, and it was a catastrophe.

Boeing commissioned a well-known University of Washington pro-
fessor, Pepper Schwartz, to come in and look at the leadership roles at
Boeing and to evaluate the health of the Boeing management structure.
Her conclusion was put very succinctly. She said Boeing has managers
by the thousands and nary a leader amongst them. And she was absolutely right, she was right on the money. In the thirty years that I have
worked at Boeing, I can honestly say that I've only encountered five
people who were actual honest-to-God leaders. The rest were manag-

ers, at best. Most of them were custodians, managerial custodians. And yet Boeing remains absolutely infatuated with the notion of leadership. They prattle on endlessly about leadership development and characteristics of a good leader and absolutely disregard all of the rhetoric that they're espousing. It's the most bizarre situation.

Premerger, most of the people who were selected really did have some technical skills. They may not have been great managers and certainly not leaders, but they had good technical skills. Postmerger, the criterion seems to have been pusillanimity, absolutely unwilling to stand up to management. The word "lickspittle" comes to mind. Let's just say obsequious.

At the corporate level it's denial and the same dysfunctional behaviors over and over again and expecting different responses. If you understand the nature of the corporation, you can actually begin to predict how they're going to react. That was one of the things that was so devastating to the workforce. Prior to the merger, the workforce understood the Boeing Company. They had a sense, an instinct about the company and how it would react in different situations. It was predictable; you may not have liked it, but you understood it. After the merger, all of that changed. Part of the angst was the breaking of the social contracts that had existed. What you had at the McDonnell Douglas Company is a group of corporate ninjas. They had continually downsized, sold off assets, made huge amounts of money for themselves and for some of their stockholders, but they decimated the company. But they'd done it profitably. So Wall Street loved them. What you had at Boeing at the time of the merger was a very collegial, bloated, flaccid management structure. When the McDonnell Douglas guys came in, they just went through them like a knife through butter—just cut their throats, hung them out to dry.

We watched and vehemently protested as the McDonnell Douglas thugs hijacked the Boeing Company and started us down the very same path that had caused the McDonnell Douglas Company to collapse into bankruptcy. We knew and actively protested the catastrophic decisions that were being made on the 787 program and were told that we were not team players, despite years of successfully leading teams on the Triple 7 and other programs. We were told that we would follow orders that we knew to be ill-advised, or we would be replaced by, quote, "someone who will." Those of us who could fought the good fight until it became apparent that it was hopeless or until our health failed, which is what happened to me. And then we retired, bitter, knowing what the future would bring and knowing that the Boeing Company that we cared so much about was doomed to failure.

After the merger, Boeing made a deliberate decision to let skills attrit out of the workforce because skills would reside at the vendors. The problem was that the vendors didn't understand how critical those skills were; nor did they want to spend the money necessary to grow those critical skills themselves. Now these skills do not exist in any-body's workforce, which is why we have problems on the 787. It's not just engineering skills. The same problems now exist in manufacturing areas. Simply put, Boeing has become irrelevant to their own products.

The 787 management decided to take on an entirely new technology for a commercial airplane, making the majority of the structure out of composite material and an entirely new manufacturing plan that not only offloads major manufacturing to other companies but also offloads engineering to partners who dearly wanted the business but were clear-ly unqualified to do the work. That was unprecedented at Boeing. Boe-ing had never left major engineering and design solely in the hands of those to whom they had outsourced manufacturing. They always had audited them to assure themselves that the companies really had the capability to meet Boeing's demand and quality schedules. They were also watched by in-house phone representatives who monitored their production and alerted Seattle to any problems. I did that kind of work for ten years when I was in international business.

Not so with the 787. Boeing trusted our partners to deliver the right parts at the right time. These stupid, stupid decisions had their roots in Phil Condit and Harry Stonecipher's so-called merger. In reality, it was a takeover of Boeing by McDonnell Douglas management. They were stupid mistakes; they were amateurish. This wasn't about a new and daunting technology that was immature. If it had been that, the prob-lem would have been very readily resolved. These were the mistakes of a company that's never built an airplane before and doesn't understand FAA compliance and the utter sanctity of configuration control. It would be the equivalent of a surgeon walking into an operating theater dressed in overalls in which he'd changed the oil of his car without washing his hands. People who know what they're doing just don't make those kinds of mistakes.

What Boeing management did is they went around to everybody, the engineers, the manufacturing people, the contracted people, and they said, "Okay, how can we save a bunch of money on this program?" And each of those departments said, "Well, you could save money if you contracted the work out." But then they were careful to say, "But you would have to have the following safeguards in place. You would have to contract out to people who knew what they were doing. You contract out in such a way that you assure configuration control compliance not only within each of the companies that you're contracting out to but between each of those companies that ship parts to each other and with us. You put quality and schedule variation processes in place to make sure the parts that people are producing are usable, that they're being produced for the cost that they say, and that they're being produced on schedule."

And each of these groups said you could save money *if* you did these things. What Boeing management did is they took that list of things and they said, "Well, all of these things you say that we need to do will cost us money, giving it to people who know how to build the parts, they're going to charge more than people who don't. Right? Why should we do that? Why should we put into place all of this configuration control stuff, we'll just make them do it. Why should we put into place verification of cost schedules and quality, that's their job, let them do it. Why should we provide them with the consulting expertise that they will need to produce this new technology?" This is all public record; it's been in the newspaper over and over and over again. They just said we're not going to take any of those precautionary measures, we're just going to give the work to people who don't know what they're doing, we're not going to verify anything, and we're not going to provide any technical expertise. It's their show.

So they lost configuration control after I and hundreds of other people had screamed about this and had been told that we weren't team players, that we didn't understand the brave new world. That we were old-timers and the McDonnell clan had a new and better way of doing business. Unfortunately, the frustration of that, I think, led directly to a number of my health problems because it just tore me up to watch it. It was like being forced to watch somebody that you love very much being raped in slow motion. At that point I just quit caring. I had to. I was tearing myself apart.

And we were dismissed. We were actively driven out and told that we weren't team players—that we were dinosaurs—that we didn't understand the future. We kept telling them, look, it's a bad plan. It isn't going to work; the 787 is not going to work. It can't. And there were hundreds of people who went to our management and pleaded, "Don't do this. You'll destroy the company." It really was like watching a catastrophic train wreck in very slow motion, wasn't it?

Now they're struggling to fix their airplanes out of sequence and have the sorriest production line of any program that Boeing has ever done. Wait until there are more airplanes in service and they start finding really serious and expensive problems. And you know, there's this duality about it that on the one hand there's a sort of perverse, "I told you so," but on the other hand, you realize that it's tens of thousands of jobs. It's a viable, vibrant American industry being destroyed. I ruined my health on it, had multiple heart attacks and some other problems that forced me to retire. It's bitterness. There's no joy in it, just a wish that they had listened. There is real outrage that they're still in denial. You just want to grab people by the lapels and say, "We've been building airplanes for eighty years, you stupid bastards! These are amateurish mistakes. And we told you. Over and over and over again." And we were run out of the company. We were sidelined. We were mothballed. We were ignored.

They don't care. They don't care. They don't care. Cause they're making money now. And what they're doing is they're saturating the market, they're selling all kinds of the old airplanes—the 737, the 747, the 767—and they're saturating the market. So in another five years the market's going to take a nosedive because it's saturated. Boeing won't have the money or the skills to develop a new product. Game over. We all know this. And the lives of so many people and families and an entire region are going to suffer for it. I had always secretly hoped after the merger, and when corporate headquarters was still in Seattle, that Airbus would buy one of those vacated buildings in Renton and open up an engineering shop within line of sight of corporate headquarters, and those guys would have eaten their hearts out over having to look out of the window and see an Airbus building. Yeah, I would have left in a heartbeat.

I still continue to fight, although I certainly don't have the investment in it that I did before, but I'm an active participant in a number of

Boeing-related online exchanges, and frankly quite well respected on many of them. Which is another thing about Boeing: you're either in or you're out. Once you leave the company, or once it's known that you were going to be laid off, you are persona non grata. People will have nothing to do with you. The only relationships that have survived have been with people that I worked on that Triple 7-300 team. That was very intense, very focused. We were called upon to resolve an entirely unanticipated problem. We did so, frankly, brilliantly. It was a unique experience. We had one of the best structural engineers in the company on the team. It involved a lot of coordination between disparate engineering and manufacturing groups. That level of understanding you only get with experience. That's why Boeing is becoming irrelevant to its own product—they are not growing those kinds of people. They've outsourced all of the work that trains people to achieve that level of understanding. They just don't exist anymore. Except the old guys, and we're retired.

CARRIE CONWAY

> Now we have men running Boeing that have never worked for Boeing. We got management in that had really no clue how the shop was run.
>
> —Hourly worker, age sixty-two, twenty-six years at Boeing,
> interviewed in 2012

I stayed home the first part of our marriage to raise kids until they got old enough to get themselves off to school, and then I did a few odd jobs. Finally decided I'd get into Boeing. Because my husband knew a lot of people, I think that helped me get into Boeing. Back then you could say, "Hey, hire this person." To be honest, I didn't want to go to Boeing because I pictured myself doing the same thing for the rest of my life, when, as it turned out, I changed jobs every five/six years and did a variety of things. You have to understand that not everybody's going to be a good fit with the Boeing Company, but it has good benefits if you can work it, stay there long enough. You have opportunity. You can practically go anyplace. As a company, I'm thankful for the wage that I got—that my husband and I got. I'm thankful for the benefits; I'm thankful for my retirement money; I'm thankful that my son has a good job; I'm thankful for what I was allowed to do.

In the early days people would meet every Friday for drinks. And sometimes I could get a babysitter. I'd go over and sit with them and talk, so I knew these people, and it really felt like I was coming home. "Oh, you're Gary's wife," and I instantly was accepted. My last year there was probably one of my best years. You talked about your family; I knew an awful lot about a lot of families. When somebody's parent died, you know, we bought cards. So you form strong friendships with a lot of people, and I really miss those friendships. Now I'm not there, and that connection is gone. There was a lot of really nice people. I had a supervisor whose son got very sick—they ended up disconnecting his life support. We talked about that. He's since retired, and so I have no connection. I ran into him at a few funerals, and he always gives me a big hug. But the friendship hasn't expanded past that.

I did a lot of work through community outreach where I raised money from various shops to buy Christmas toys. I was in the Five Building when I started the first real community outreach program, adopt a family, and I ran that for my area. In fact, I had a bucket. We get paid on Thursday, so Friday I'd walk around with my bucket asking for change. I don't remember now how many thousands of dollars—I have it written down someplace. We divided up everybody who wanted to go shopping—we'd got a family, it was a woman raising her grandchildren, and she's dying of cancer; son of the father is trying to get out of prison so he can come home, and they had nothing. Boy, we just inundated them with things that they needed; we went shopping for clothes, food, filled the pantries up with food, had sacks of flour, sugar, and clothes, bikes. I can't tell you how much, but every dime we spent—we spent like a thousand dollars on blankets and pillows and that sort of thing. We spent a thousand dollars on coats and hats, different sizes. And when I was in the Six Building, the first three years that I was there, twice a month we put lunches on. We'd buy the food, make the food, put barbeques on, collect the money, and then we'd buy toys for Toys for Tots.

Boeing has changed over the years. It's not a family. I asked my son up in the Six Building, "Did you do anything for Toys for Tots?" "Oh, if we want to." I said, "So nobody's running anything?" "No." How sad. Boeing is a big company with a lot of people with heart, or used to be. I think it's not all management's fault, not by any means. I think a lot of the people that came in were just not interested in even getting to know the workers around you. But it's sad. It is sad that that building went that way. When I was doing potlucks, we had two other people that helped me all the time, but when they got transferred out, nobody would really step up. You can't do a potluck for that big a building without help, and I got help for Christmas. So I'm sad that building deteriorated that much. It's no longer a family.

From the day I hired in, this is where Boeing is, this is where home is. When upper Boeing closed up the headquarters and shipped it to Chicago, and when Boeing bought McDonnell Douglas—actually McDonnell Douglas bought Boeing—they moved the president of McDouglas into upper management at the Boeing Company. Things started changing right from the get-go when he moved in. Now we have men running Boeing that have never worked for Boeing. We got management in that had no clue how the shop was run. When they came in, they tried to change things, or if things weren't looking good for them, they rush in with snap judgments and try to change things. It got worse as time went on closer to my retirement: they would try to fix what was wrong in their area by pushing the problem further down into somebody else's area. Do the best you can and move it down the line, which then became another manager's job to fix. And that was happening a lot. How can they understand what we do—what kind of a company we are—if you've never worked for the company? You didn't grow up through the ranks and learn what the company was all about. You know, not a clue. After they bought McDonnell Douglas, we started calling it McBoeing. We knew McDonnell Douglas people were coming in, and they would change it; that was the start of the change. So not the same company. The new ones don't know that culture.

You know the problems of the '87? One day I'm working, and my lead brought all the parts out of storage. They were all wrapped up in paper, brown paper. This was on a Monday morning, so all the tables were stacked with the necessary parts to do whatever we were working on. So I started unwrapping mine, and you can see chips in it, little tiny holes. And there were areas where you could tell corrosion—corrosion has a different look to it. So the first part I took to my lead, and I said, "Look at this." He said, "Oh, can't use that." Well, it took four parts to get one that I could use. When the inspector came in, I called him over—I'd saved one of them. I said, "I want you to look at this part," and he goes, "Well, that's not acceptable," and I said, "Well, we got a whole warehouse full of them, you know. I had to get to the fourth part to find an acceptable one." He went into the warehouse, started checking all these parts, and he came back and stopped production. He figured about two-thirds of this order was pitted and corroded. Before the day was over, his boss and my boss were standing on one side of the table. My inspector and I were standing on the other side of the table. My boss was telling me I have to use these parts, and both of us said, "No, we're not doing that." It took months. I'm not even sure when, because I ended up getting transferred out of the building over it.

I found a part that had bird shit on it. Now, these parts are supposed to be made in a clean environment—not supposed to be outside. We weren't allowed to bring anything to eat or put in our mouth; we had to wear gloves all the time. It was a clean building. So I took this part, and I said, "Hey, how'd this get there? I unwrapped the brown paper from it." The country and everything, it's so different than ours. They didn't understand why we were so picky. It didn't mean anything to them.

But I think the airplane [787] looks very nice; it's obviously selling, and now Airbus is having problems—yay (laughs). I'm glad they finally got it in the air. They're not having a huge amount of problems with it now. They've fixed, and are still continuing to fix, whatever problems they come up with. So, you know, it's like one step ahead into the future, which a lot of times that means one step further away from the past.

I would hope a few would say I'd be missed, missed as a person. But when my husband and I walked around and said good-bye, I got a lot of hugs. I got a lot of "Boy, we're going to miss you. Who's going to do this now," that sort of thing. I did my best. They could depend on me to be there. Maybe I made a difference in some of my coworkers' lives, just by being, just by talking to them and laughing with them.

Part II

Still Employed at Boeing

Even though stories from retired Boeing workers provide a vivid point of reference against which current-day employees judge their present conditions, it may be tempting to discount retired workers' memories as rosy, selective, and even inaccurate portrayals of the company and their own work experiences. Or perhaps retirees seem frozen in time: now that they no longer contend with the ins and outs of daily work life, they do not confront coping with, making sense of, or accepting Boeing's new organizational ethos. They have the luxury of living within, or remaining rooted within, the Boeing of yesteryear. Their reactions to this new business culture are idiosyncratic to their cohort and portend little about the ways in which today's workers regard their employment. What about those who lived through the changes we have described and continue to work for Boeing? Do we see differences in their loyalty? In the ways they find work to be meaningful? In their levels of emotional or mental investment in their work or how they understand the tacit contract they have with their employer? It is the stories of these long-tenured, continuing employees we hear in this second section.

As one would expect, these continuing employees who, like the retirees, lived through Boeing's organizational change are predictably different on some demographic factors; our 1997 survey data show that this cohort's average age was forty (compared to age fifty-six for those who would be in our retiree cohort in 2011), and they had worked at Boeing for an average of thirteen years (compared to twenty years for the retirees). On many indicators we find that they are more similar to than different from the retirees. Continuing employees were roughly the same as retirees on absenteeism and on some questions dealing with their commitment to the company and optimism about the company's future. They also believed that labor unions could be counted on to protect American workers at roughly the same rates (53 versus 57 percent). These two cohorts also had nearly identical views on what they thought the company owed them in terms of pay, benefits, and advancement opportunities, suggesting that they both subscribed to the balanced exchanges embodied in the traditional forms of the social contract.

When we look at the survey data from 2006, however, a more interesting picture begins to emerge, one that points to a slow, perhaps almost imperceptible shift that is also mirrored in the narratives we present in this second section. For example, to the question "I would turn down another job with more pay to stay at Boeing," only 21 percent of the continuing employees agreed, as compared to 30 percent for those who would be retired in 2011. Similarly, only 20 percent of the continuing employees thought that "Boeing really cares about my well-being" (versus 32 percent who would be retired by 2011), and 50 percent of the continuing employees agreed that "Top management doesn't understand my job" (compared with 40 percent). Although many continuing employees (48 percent) disagreed with the statement "I feel very little loyalty to Boeing," this number was much less than that of the soon-to-retire workers (60 percent). Questions related to involvement and engagement with their work also suggested a decline. For example, to the statement "I show up early for work to get things ready," 54 percent of continuing employees agreed, but this was significantly less than the 67 percent of soon-to-be-retired workers who endorsed it. Similarly, 48 percent of the retired agreed with the statement "Most things in life are more important than work," but this was considerably less than the 64 percent of continuing employees who agreed. The ways in which these two cohorts perceived risk to the company's future also varied, with continuing employees reporting more than the retirees that outsourcing, subcontracting, and inability to hold market share posed a threat.

Without question, there is no single item, no single response, that provides a clear-cut basis for delineating a point in time to mark when the company changed. Rather, the set of responses over time reflects that something meaningful has occurred. In a similar manner, the employees themselves show a range of reaction. To be sure, some of the narratives in this section illustrate views of work and the company that are reminiscent of Heritage Boeing days. Some of the remarks from female employees highlight the positive changes the company has made regarding how women are treated in what had been, and still remains, a largely male-dominated company. Many, however, are highly critical of company actions and have grown more distant, detached, and instrumental as a result.

We acknowledge that some of the changes we find might be more *age* rather than *cohort* related. Perhaps it has always been the case that, irrespective of decade or century, workers approaching retirement become more invested, more loyal, and more trusting. Taken as a whole, however, these narrative patterns disclose a gradual shifting, one that reflects a critical unraveling of time-honored, vital orientations workers have had toward their employers. These shifting patterns have also been noted by other scholars and writers in the popular press who have observed declining loyalties, trust, and engagement between "baby boomers" and "Gen X" employees. Although there is debate as to the strength of such generational differences, baby boomers (born between 1946 and 1964) have been described as possessing a stronger work ethic, placing work above personal life, and being less likely to challenge authority than Gen Xers (born between 1965 and 1982).[1] Indeed, the changes at Boeing are consistent with these broader trends and employees' experiences in other US companies. Whether such changes are attributable principally to broader historical, cultural, or social movements or to one's firsthand experiences cannot be discerned neatly. Both likely play an important role. For in these narratives, we hear how employees' experiences shape their understanding of this more widespread changing employment landscape as well as how their personal experiences confirm and validate that which they read in the news.

4

STILL FAMILY

Business consultants and scholars extol the virtues of committed and engaged employees for the health of corporate America. Such employees quit less often, perform better at their jobs, and often go the extra mile for the company. This chapter highlights five individuals who embody many of these characteristics, as well as elements of the older-style social contract between employees and companies. These employees talk about their work with airplanes with enthusiasm and passion. Their loyalty to Boeing is grounded in their deep identification with the company and in their appreciation of what the company has provided for them. Two explicitly acknowledge Boeing's central role in their personal development. Jessica Worth, for example, describes how she "was raised Boeing" as she matured from being "just a baby" when she started as a twenty-year-old to becoming a "mom" or "grandma" to her engineers years later. Another marks significant events in his life, such as marriages and deaths, by what he was doing in the company, noting that the company "shapes who you are."

All of these employees, in their own ways, appreciate what Boeing offers them. Jim Sidwell and Drew King explicitly contrast the benefits of working at Boeing with how things "suck" out in the "real world." Boeing seems to become a safe haven for this group—a place to stay for your whole career or to return to if you should be unlucky enough to end up in the cutthroat economy "out there." Indeed, one longtime engineer believes Boeing has a "lot of soul" because it cares about and values its employees. This group reciprocates by "going beyond": staying late, finding ways to save time or money on work processes, never taking a day of sick leave, or worrying about "idiot" workers who text while walking in front of an airplane on the flight line, lose their legs, and cause Boeing trouble with the Department of Labor and Industries. One recounts telling her husband and son that "Boeing gets the best of me," while they get "the worst of me because I am so tired when I get home." This dedication and involvement with their work is not just a response to Boeing's perceived benevolence. Each is genuinely engrossed by the challenges of his or her job, the need to solve problems creatively, and the drive to work cooperatively with others. But their deep identification with Boeing certainly contributes.

The pride this group has in the company does not mean these individuals are blind to the problems or mistakes Boeing has made. They are fully aware, for example, of the problems with the 787 business model. However, these and other gripes they may have (and for this group there are few) do not destroy or even shake their deep affection for and pride in the company. Some acknowledge the problems but blame "them," the alien McDonnell Douglas management that intruded into Boeing and tried to destroy the heritage culture. Others accentuate the positive and minimize the problems, as when, for example, Ron Norbert and Rita Haynes focus on the exhilaration of watching the 787 first take flight rather than on the long delay and cost overruns. Similarly, Drew King accepts the opening of a second assembly line for the 787 in South Carolina by noting that the Puget Sound region doesn't have the capacity. At least the jobs are going to American workers, he reasons. Even a three-year layoff does not sour Jim Sidwell's view of the company. The layoff becomes a "blessing" because it enabled him to spend more time with his family.

RON NORBERT

> But I chose Boeing way back, and so that's who I am. I'm going to be a retired Boeing engineer.
> —Engineer, age sixty-seven, over forty years at Boeing,
> interviewed in 2012

I started work at Boeing in June 1968 in the materials technology group in Lynwood, Washington. Boeing got me a deferment. From week to week I didn't know if I was going to be drafted. But the deferment held, so I didn't ever go in the service. I did try to spend some time on the aerospace side to help out the armed forces. In early 1979 I was chosen to work on the 767 being designed in Italy. I worked there for two years—great experience in Torino and traveling to the Naples area. The only rough part was having to go to work every day, every week. Actually that was good, the work was interesting—a really good job. I was recently married, so it was kind of a honeymoon for two years. Toward the end of the stay there, I got a security questionnaire. I wasn't sure where it would lead. I think it was in late '81 that I was asked to report to a program. I was guessing it might be the so-called black hole at the developmental center, south Boeing Field, in the old supersonic transport building. I worked there for nine years. We couldn't tell anybody where we worked. It later came out that it was the B-2 bomber program. The stay in Italy was maybe the most fun, but as a program, the B-2 was probably the most interesting and best program I was ever on. Today I still work with people that I worked with there.

The B-2 program was top secret and wasn't known about until 1988, at the rollout. Of course, at that time the standard answer was "It's just a company proprietary program." We had what we called the "hello phone," so when we'd answer the phone, we didn't say any program, like today you might say, "Materials technology." You just said, "Hello" (laughs). There was a lot of funny things about the B-2 program. It was officially "Project Wilo." I don't know if anyone knew exactly what it meant, but it was said to be that T. A. Wilson, who was still the president when that program started, he thought it was just his name with some letters after it. No one was ever quite sure. We worked in a shuttered building with no daylight. You entered through airlock doors; there were double doors that you went through, so someone walking by the front of the building could not see into the building. So it came to be known as "What's it like outside" (laughs). It took about six to eight months for someone chosen to get cleared into the program, and once you're there, it seemed like you really had accomplished something. It was "Gee whiz," you know, "this is an amazing airplane program," and so it was. Boeing was building portions of it—composite materials—and it was really a pretty advanced program.

It was a very close-knit group—just a wonderfully cooperative group. I was really proud to be working for the company. It was the most creative time. Everybody really pitched in to get the job done. In the materials technology group, there were probably twenty or twenty-five. The only people you could talk to about anything were in the program, so that made it all the more close. I have a lot of B-2 memorabilia. I've even got the certificate for weight-saving contributor of the year. We got quite a prize from the company for that: a company-paid trip to Colorado. That was pretty neat. Of course, I was kind of incognito through the eighties, while I was on the program. Really didn't do anything but go to work and come home. I didn't even go to other Boeing buildings very often.

I had a brother and a sister who passed away during the program. I had to spend some time in Portland where my sister lived when she was dying of lung cancer. I spent a couple of one-week periods taking care of her. Then I had another death in the family. The company was pretty understanding. They allowed me to go down there. Take as much time as you need, get things straightened out. I think I kind of just put my head down and got through it. It was not particularly pleasant at times by any means, but, yeah, I just want to underscore the understanding of the management was wonderful, really they were. There was no demand that I had to be back to work at a certain time or anything. Boeing has a nice tradition: if there's a death in the family, there's a card that all the coworkers sign. I had one the other day for someone whose father passed away. Well, all of my family has passed away while I've worked for Boeing, so I've gotten those cards a number of times. Yeah, coworkers are always very supportive. It's a wonderful group of people working there. You couldn't ask for a better group to work with.

I went on the 787 program sometime in '03 or '04, I think. They worked on building a list of standard parts to reduce the inventory for the program and save costs. I worked on that a couple of years, and then I was asked to go back to Italy. Italy was one of our partners on the 787. It was a really wonderful year. We had a lot of troubles with that particular partner in Italy, but I firmly believe they're getting quite a bit better. My feeling [about the 787 program] was that they did not use some of the lessons learned from earlier programs. I was one who actually worked abroad on the first program, the 767, and the Italians and the Japanese both were doing design work. The design work was done there, but we had Boeing people in oversight positions. That was the thing they did not do nearly adequately on the 787, there's no doubt about it in my mind. Having seen how one of them worked, not to say we didn't have troubles on 767, we did, but it just only underscored the fact you had to have a lot more oversight. I think that's what the upper management has come to see.

It's not so bad to give things to foreign countries; Boeing has always had to do what they term "offset programs," where they give work to the countries that buy the airplanes. They share some of the work, and that makes some sense, I think. But on the '87, of course, they put out a lot more than they ever had before. Designed somewhere else, and it was only being assembled here. Everybody on the 787 program has to work with foreign engineers; that's the job. They're harder to understand. And we worked with people from all over the world on this program, more so than in the past, but we always have had some of that. It's part of the culture of the company to work with other countries on these things, but in this one, I think they went overboard. Frankly, my belief is that it wasn't the same Boeing anymore; it was actually, well, you've heard the term McBoeing? There was the McDonnell aircraft element. McDonnell Douglas had tried this with China before, where they pretty much put an entire airplane in China. I think Boeing was trying not to use its own money on the 787, recognizing it was going to be really expensive. It turned out to be really expensive for Boeing as well as all the partners, and later than any Boeing product has ever been.

The rollout was pretty neat. They even had the Italians dedicate the building. They had the bishop come and say mass inside. Of course, most Italians are Catholic. Actually, I am too. So I even got to carry the offerings up along with an Italian woman. My son always says if we weren't German we'd be Italian. So that was pretty neat from what I remember. But I didn't realize how bad things were. We were shipping some of the stuff, but we knew there were temporary hold fasteners on these things. I had no idea things were so bad.

For a company so large, I think they have a lot of soul. I know that retirees continue to have a real love for the company. Some of them more than others maybe, but one of my closest friends lives in southern Oregon, and I think that many of his friends are friends from Boeing—they're lifelong friends. I'd definitely promote Boeing to anyone who wanted to go there. They value people to a high degree because the people are actually the real value of the company, not the bricks and

mortar. It sounds cliché, and I know it gets repeated in their presenta-
tions. They have excellence hours and things like that where a lot of that
comes up, but I think it's really true. I guess I'd like to believe that the
management feels that way too, that people are the real value, because
without an innovative and creative and dedicated staff of people, they
simply couldn't build the products they do. It's said that these airplanes
are just a collection of parts flying in close formation. The products are
immense works, really technical works, and without the people they
simply couldn't be done, no matter how many factories or other things
they have. So I think they treat the people very well.

I've tried to be a good employee, from being on time to trying to
complete assignments on schedule. I've tried to go beyond; even today,
I know that if I'm ready to head for home and someone calls from the
shop, I'm not going to go home. I'm going to stay there and help. I think
some of it is setting an example for younger employees too. The pay's
important, for sure, and the travel has been wonderful. That was a side
benefit that I never foresaw. But no, it's a lot more than that, I think: I
think it shapes who you are. I would be a quite different person if I
hadn't worked at Boeing, if I'd worked at some other job, even if in
engineering. But I chose Boeing way back, and so that's who I am. I'm
going to be a retired Boeing engineer. That's the way I describe myself.
Not just a retired person but a retired Boeing engineer.

DREW KING

> Being a machinist is a part of me, just like being Norwegian German
> is a part of me.
>   —Machinist, age fifty-five, thirty-four years at Boeing,
>   interviewed in 2011

My mom and dad worked at Boeing before I was born, and my uncle
and cousin worked there too. When I got out of the navy, I built houses
for a year, but within months I applied for the four-year machinist
apprenticeship program at Boeing. When I went through the apprenticeship, I ran practically every machine in the shop. I love building. I
just love working with my hands. I make parts for the Triple 7, and we
do about seven and a half, eight of those planes a month. Right now
we're a couple lines ahead, and we can do a line in three days. So we're

always ahead, but there's always something to work on. When we get slow on machinist work, I go out and ask a few people whether they need something moved, or bubble wrap taken somewhere, and/or we get sent to another area to burr parts; yeah, we're always kind of behind on burring parts.

[On slow days] some people take vacations because they just don't want to burr parts or mop floors. None of that bothers me. I just have a boss that says, "You're like a kid with ADD—if you're not working you're out." I just like to stay moving. You're always looking at ways to make that part faster. Right now we're trying to even out our run time; we're trying to get twenty-nine minutes down to twenty-two. Money is time, and time is money. I'm not a programmer, but you can still find ways to maybe use a different cutter that will cut material off faster or stuff like that. We can come up with the idea.

We do ninety-eight holes in these things called crossbeams, and the holes have to be within one-sixth of the diameter of your hair. Your hair is three-thousandths of an inch thick. Well, we hold it to one-half of one-thousandth. If it gets oversized, then it has to go to engineering to see if we can use that hole being oversized. So my parts when they're completed—I think they average about $2,700. There are cheaper ones, and there are a lot more expensive ones. There are some $35,000 parts in our shop, depending on the material. Titanium material is expensive. Makes me feel good that I can do that. Probably fifteen, twenty years ago, we really didn't know what the cost of our parts was. So it's good that they've got that under control, so to speak, and it's nice to know, "Gosh, I'm working on a $2,000 part. I better ask one more question before I push go."

Computers weren't around when I started; everything was punch card. Now there are so many computers in the shop. When I was going through the apprenticeship, I ran the first NC machine where it actually takes the tool out of the spindle, switches it around, puts in a new tool, and puts this one away. I'm thinking, "GOSH MAN, I didn't have to touch nothing!" You start out with tapes that you have to load into the machine, and now you just download something. In thirty-four years it's amazing how far we've come. You know if we don't do it, other people are. So we better be doing it. We're still a very important part, even though machines are all automated. I guess when things were more manual, you had more of a fingerprint on it. You don't have that quite as much. Even though I don't program parts, I can think of a cutter that maybe will do something better or faster rather than a 4 flute. So yes, you have a lot of opportunity to improve stuff even though machines are more automated. Things can't stay the same, or else we'd still be covering our wings with fabric.

The main or constant downside is dealing with people who aren't quite like you. Nothing against females, but this female that came over—she just doesn't run like me. She'll sit there and do the Internet thing. She makes rock jewelry, so she's constantly on the Internet looking at beads. She'll even start weaving gold chains and polishing rocks, but then she'll say in the crew meeting, "We have to do something with machine 3 because I just don't have time to sit down." Yes, you do. The guy I work with will always ask me, "Where's your girlfriend at?" And I'm like, "I don't know. I thought she was your girlfriend! Next time you guys go out to dinner, will you ask her where she goes all day long?" Yeah, so that's my kind of day. We try to have fun and be safe.

Being a machinist is a part of me, just like being Norwegian German is a part of me. Well, I guess you have to take me at my word, but I'm a hard worker. I'm a very conscientious go-getter. Not that Boeing would fall apart if I missed a week. You know what I mean. I'm the guy that likes to go to work, do my job, and I don't care what goes on behind the scenes, so to speak. I volunteer for extra stuff—family day I stay out after to get that ready. We used to support the troops: we would make a lot of money for holiday families, but that became a conflict of interest because we make military parts. [Since] this second guy level came in, we haven't had a single fund-raiser, but the two years that we did, me and another person went out and bought all the stuff that the troops could use—Silly String so they could shoot it, toothpaste, cards, candy so they could give it out to the kids. Anyways, twice I hauled out over nine hundred pounds of stuff out to Ellensburg, which is 130 miles away, to give to a bigger organization where they box it up and send it out. So I like that. I don't think I worked at Boeing for more than a month when they came around and said, "We're having a blood drive. Would you like to donate?" And I said, "Sure!" I don't know why I said yes, but that day I donated, and I think I have half a gallon to go and then I'll be up to eighteen gallons of blood—124 holes in each arm.

I used to say that I was proud to work at Boeing early on, and I wouldn't mind wearing my badge—accidentally usually. You know, you would go to the grocery store, oh man, so you put it in your pocket. [Now] sometimes I'm embarrassed to say where I work, mainly because of the change of management. Negative changes seem to be getting more noticeable. For example, they hire younger people that don't have machine shop experience. We've a got twenty-six-year-old girl, or twenty-seven-year-old girl/guy as managers, and, you know, when you're used to the last twenty-eight out of thirty-four years of having management that grew up in Boeing or grew up in the shops and they know how to machine. . . . Some of these new managers tell you, "We're not supposed to be machinists. We're supposed to manage processes and people." Well, I'm sorry. They don't do that very well either. My machine had a big crash a couple of weeks ago. So a female supervisor said, "Can you explain what happened?" And I said, "Yeah, the 'way' covers jammed up and pushed out the weld." And wait, what are "way" covers? And I just . . . that kills me. To have to explain to my supervisor simple stuff like that. They say we're the experts and we do the work, but they don't seem to listen very much to the people on the shop floor that actually do the work.

They need to get new people in here, and they've really let the apprenticeship go way down. Well, now you're starting to see apprentices in the shop. They need skilled workers. I'm not all about money. I think now they're starting wages at $12 or $13. Some of these younger kids might think, "God, we're driving out to Everett for $14 and gas— you could work down home for $10," and they don't see the benefit of medical insurance, maybe because they're not old like me. Like this one lady, her daughter worked at an espresso stand. She's making good money there but no benefits—no sick leave, no nothing. I think people that are within maybe five or ten years of retiring are maybe a little bit happier than some of the younger people are. Gosh, I hate to sound like my parents (laughs). You know, I started working at $6.36 an hour. I think this younger generation is more of an "I want" generation, and it's funny to see some of these kid supervisors walking around. It's just amazing. They wear their pants baggy just like if you saw them out on the street. You'd think when they got a job and they were management, they'd pull them up and wear a belt or something (laughs). It's just weird. When I first started, the manager had to wear a tie and, you know, slacks. Now basically they can wear t-shirts and jeans, baggy jeans, tennis shoes.

I've been on five or six strikes in thirty-four years. You can't make everybody happy all the time. There's some people that I think they live in a cave. You can sit back and say, "Well, it would sure be nice to have another three days of vacation or two more days of bereavement leave, or a little bit better retirement." If they knew what other people were making . . . you know? I kind of got in an argument with a guy once. I'm going to guess he's thirty-eight, forty years old, and I said, "You add up the pros and the cons. You go ask people that actually don't work at Boeing about their benefits and then you look at yours, and you tell me which are better." We didn't talk for a couple months. Sure, there are people out there that make a lot more than us, but there's a lot of people out there that are still looking for a job.

Well, I could be more upset they're building the 787 in South Carolina, but in my opinion there's no way we can build that many planes ourselves. So if we're going to have somebody else do it, I'd rather have somebody in our country do it. They learned their lesson because of the three-year delay in the 787, of having so many people have so much input and not have very much control over it. The fifty-eight-day strike did *not* delay that airplane three years. And they [top management] admit that to us—maybe a little bit to the public—but whenever you hear about that, the first thing [mentioned] is our strike. So I don't mind seeing somebody in another state help us out building the airplanes, not at all.

I think Boeing is a good company. You know, none of us liked it when Boeing moved to Chicago. It's a Seattle company, but they wanted to be amongst taller buildings, with bigger bigwigs and stuff like that. And then when plant two was torn down, it was like, "Man, that's where Boeing started." But I'm still proud to work at Boeing. I wouldn't have what I have now without it. You know, I couldn't have what I have today from working at a gas station or McDonald's. Boeing used to be called the Lazy B. That's not the case anymore, and maybe it wasn't ever; it wasn't ever for me. I didn't go there so I could be a part of the Lazy B group. I tell people I'd rather work somewhere for $15 for a job I love than $25 for a job I don't. No matter what you select, make sure you like it or love it. Only reason I don't spring out of bed like I'm spring-loaded is because of my back, because I used to pop right out of bed. I was out of bed before the alarm was completely shut off. I always looked forward to going to work.

JIM SIDWELL

> I think the longer I go and the more I see of the company, I see what
> a great entity it is.
> —Mechanic in his midforties, twenty years at Boeing,
> interviewed in March 2012

I hired in as a preflight delivery mechanic in Everett. My crew takes the airplane from the paint hangar; we do fueling functional tests—putting the fuel in, checking all the tubing, getting it down the engine, making sure everything works correctly, there's no leak, pressure-testing the tanks, that type of thing. Then we run the engines, check all the flight controls, make sure they all work correctly. And there's things that break, there's troubleshooting, there's component replacement. Next is fly the plane; we don't, there's flight crews who do it, but we fix anything that they find discrepant. After that is customer walk, and that's where the customer gets the airplane for a day, and they get to play with it, they get to walk through it, check it out, and then after they fly it, they take delivery of it.

Safety is a very big concern with the Boeing Company; when I hired in, it really wasn't talked about as much. This crew I'm on now, we've jelled, and we're really, really a tight crew. It's a team that, despite the cliché "the Lazy B," we work well together. If you get a good crew like mine, you watch out for each other, and you watch for those who come in the stall that don't have a clue and shouldn't be on the flight line. Cause it can be a dangerous place. You can get seriously hurt. A couple weeks ago, at night, there was a guy carelessly walking along—one of our policies is when an airplane has no power, we have what's called "chock walkers." The big tug pulls the airplane, and you have a person on each wing tip, a person on the tail, and a person at the nose, and then you have one person on either side, one for each main landing gear who are carrying chocks, to chock the tires, in case the airplane stops or the tow bar breaks, so you can stop it. So he's got this chock, and he's walking along texting and gets in front of the tires and the thing ate him; it knocked him down, ran over him. He lost both legs from below the knees. It was at night during second shift, and, yeah, it messed that guy; I think he was in his thirties. Talk about life altering, and of course to me this guy was an idiot. What are you doing walking in front of an airplane and texting? You know, come on, put it away. And the sad thing is, the Boeing Company will pay through the nose for that guy's stupidity. We see it a lot, how people abuse the Boeing Company.

There are times the stress level is through the roof. I mean, we have our problems, like a fly date, when we're trying to fly the airplane. Things can go sideways in a hurry; customer will lock a delivery, an FAA ticket, they're pretty tense, and you've got to be on the ball, you've got to jump through hoops, you've got to get stuff done. That's where the professionalism of my crew will come together, and it's like, okay, no BS, let's do this. It can get stressful and tense. At the end of the day at 2:30, when I punch the time clock and I leave and walk out, it's done, it's over; I don't carry it with me.

I take pride in my work and take a lot of pride in saying, "I work for the Boeing Company." It's a great company, and it goes back to those junior guys who come in with their hand out thinking they're owed more; it's like, "No, you're not." I think the longer I go and the more I see of the company, I see what a great entity it is. They really do take care of their people. For example, all the chemicals that we have to deal with—I mean, it's nasty stuff. There are known carcinogens. When I first hired in and the company didn't really care and we got sealant on our hands and we'd use MEK, which if I took a thimble of MEK, dumped it in your palm, wiped it off, you would taste it in less than a minute. I worked with a guy that was pulled over going home; the cop thought that he had been drinking, gave him a Breathalyzer, and he blew positive from the chemicals he was working with. He said, "No, I haven't been drinking," and he ended up not getting a ticket, but this stuff goes right into your body. That was 1988. Now we have all the PPE, personal protective equipment, available to us, so if you're getting sick because of the chemicals you're using, it's your own fault.

The very first flight of the 747-400 was a big deal, and I was a big part of that. The 777, when it first came out, I wasn't working on it, but, you know, it was just as amazing, it's my company. I know everybody working on it. New programs are exciting but also a pain because you start from scratch. The 787 was extremely painful because the company tried too many new things at one time. It would have been really nice if the company came down to talk to the people that build the airplane. This is what we're thinking. But as far as gratification goes, yeah, watching them fly, that's the ultimate, that's why we're doing it.

The 787, I was nervous, really nervous about that one. That first one that flew, I was on that crew, I was on that first one, and it was coming down and getting crunch time to make it fly, and we're already late, we're, what, two years late to make it fly and, I mean, we have it ready to go, we have the crew coming out, and then we're told, "No, we're not flying because there's some engineering thing, we found a fault, we found something that needs to be fixed." And we're, "Fly it, it'll fly, it'll do it." And you know, we, as the workers, the mechanics, the electricians, the avionics, the technicians, everybody involved, we all knew it would fly. "Fly it, it'll do it." But no, we had to take it apart, rebuild it, put it back together, and then it flew. It's been flying flawlessly; it's got issues, it's got growing pains, but yeah, you know, to see it fly, that's why we're doing it.

Regrets? No, no, not at all. I wish I wasn't laid off for a few years in between, but it gave me time with my family, and it was a blessing.

RITA HAYNES

When I joined Boeing, it was cool, it was always fun, and even up to this day, like when the 777 first flew or when the 787 first flew, I get teary eyed watching the whole thing (laughs). It's amazing.
—Engineer, unknown age, sixteen years total at Boeing, interviewed in 2012

I grew up just loving science and math, loved traveling, loved airplanes; they always gave me the butterflies. From the start, I wanted to study aerodynamics, but I also liked the arts. My mom wanted me to go study art in Paris; the more she pushed, the more I leaned towards engineering. From the beginning, I loved airplanes; they are my passion. When I joined Boeing, it was cool, it was always fun, and even up to this day, like when the 777 first flew or when the 787 first flew, I get teary eyed watching the whole thing (laughs). It's amazing.

I started back in the 1980s. I'm an aerospace engineer by trade; I had a friend who got a job at Boeing and gave me some names and contacts. I called them up and sent my resume. Anyway, long story short, I got a job offer on the phone, and so they moved me over here. I started out in research. I did a lot of computational fluid dynamics; it is the computer modeling of wings and airflows around them, that type of thing. I changed jobs a lot. I went from research to performance engineering and ended up working on the 777 design. I was on the team that worked on the wing design from an aero perspective. I went back to school with Boeing's help and got my MBA. Later I switched to marketing, working with airlines in the Middle East, Europe, and North America. After a while, I went back to engineering in middle management. I had many people reporting to me. I did that for a while and then left the company. By then I had two kids, so I decided to take some time off to raise my family.

After ten years I decided it was time to go back. My philosophy is just take chances, so I did. I like to have fun at my work, and I like to learn new things and do different things. As a result, I haven't been at the same job for too long. But I think that's why I like Boeing, because it gives me that opportunity to bounce around, grow, and spread the knowledge.

I love working with people; I enjoy them. One thing I do at work is I don't take things personally; for me, it's business. Sometimes, it gets pretty tense. Campaigns get tough, people are working a lot, there's stress, the higher-ups, everybody's demanding something different, so the stress level can really go through the ceiling for a lot of these people, and they just lose it. You have to be able to stay focused on the end goal and keep it going. After ten years, I could have gone somewhere else, but I came back to Boeing. It's a great company, and the people make it fun, they really do.

We just went and visited my nephew's son; this little guy, you know, he's all about airplanes. So I took him all this Boeing stuff to give him and inspire him. He was all excited. "Come on up," I told him, "I'll take you around." It's an amazing industry to be in, and it's so different than everything else, and yet the company's so big you can do just about anything you want. When you see an airplane, like the 787 with all its growing pains, finally fly, it's like, "Hey, this really came together." That is the most gratifying moment.

My biggest challenge was I did not want to get a job because I was a female. I wanted to get a job based on my qualifications. The funniest part is the first day I reported to work, I didn't have the pass to get in. So I knocked on the door, waited for a while, and finally somebody came. I said, "I'm just reporting today, this is my first day." So he walked me in, and said, "Oh, I think this is your area." He put me in the office administrator desk because he probably thought, "Hey, female, young, there she goes." So I waited and waited, and finally the manager who hired me showed up; he starts taking me around. I can see the look on these people's faces, especially the guy who just sat me down. It was kind of humorous, but I worked with all older guys, my dad's age. That was a bit awkward at first; I got used to it.

Sometimes you get challenged: "Oh, you got it just because you're a female." Not as much anymore, but in the earlier days a lot, and when I went to the flight line, it was tough with a bunch of guy mechanics, even though they have female mechanics; it's tough when they see a female manager. But I managed. There's always a couple that give you the once-over, challenge everything you say. It was a little bit of that, but nothing that I would lose sleep over. There was only one boss where I didn't feel valued, but for most of my career at Boeing, I have been. I felt valued, obviously in the paycheck, but the verbal thank-you, an acknowledgment, that's all I need that I did a good job.

For me, the ten years I took time off . . . I don't have any regret over taking that time off. Going back, seeing everybody's faces ten years older, yeah, they recognize me, but I wasn't sure who was who anymore. There was a lot of paper processing before; all of that was computer now, you know, so the technology had changed in ten years, but Boeing was still Boeing; the people were still the same. I wish I didn't have to restart, but in hindsight, things being the way they were, I would still do the same.

JESSICA WORTH

> I feel like I've just grown up here. I was raised Boeing.
> —Office employee, age fifty-two, thirty-one years at Boeing,
> interviewed in 2012

I graduated from college back in 1980 with a degree in accounting. I was only twenty, and my sister worked here, so she found out about a couple jobs, and I interviewed. I loved it from first day. I started right in, and I hired into a group called Airplane Safety on the 767 program. One of the main things I did in my job was input accidents and incidents into our database, and it was for all of Boeing airplanes as well as

Airbus airplanes. If it was just an event like a bird strike or something like that, then it was called an "event and incident." I was the office administrator for the whole group, so if anybody should have been scared to fly, it should have been me. But it didn't seem to deter me at all. You know, I guess because I realized that what I was seeing was only the bad things and that you know there was millions of flights that were happening where none of this stuff happens. It's just the way it is. It's safer to fly in an airplane than it is to ride in a car. But I still love it. I was in that job for eleven years, and now I've been in Noise, Vibrations and Emissions engineering for a little over twenty years.

I am on computer now, so I do any kind of correspondence that they need, coordination sheets. I do releases of information. I work with a lot of PhDs in my group and any papers that they have to present at a conference or whatever. I have to go through and get all the way to the vice president to get approvals for the release of information, and then I have to go through export control and intellectual properties and finally through communications to get these released. So I spend a lot of time doing those kinds of things, and then setting up meetings is a huge thing—trying to find conference rooms. Oh gosh. I spend a lot of time organizing the activities in the group. I maintain all the instant recognitions through our group—so all the gifts. We have like $10 gifts we give out to people. When they bring people in to interview for a job, I take care of that process where I find out when they are going to be able to come in for the interview and then set up hotels for them and a car and their air tickets and all that kind of stuff and then do a lot of expense reports. Probably my main job here is travel. With all the engineers I support, and they travel all the time, I set up all their travel and the hotels, and, like I said, the cars and all that and then do all their expense reports when they come back. That is the good thing about being here this many years. If I don't know the answer myself, I know who to go to get it. I've always been really busy at my job here, and I like that. I like working with the engineers and like keeping busy. I call myself the mother. I am the mother of all because they come to me for everything, and I feel like I have a really close bond with all of them. They are really good guys. I support two hundred people with my job now, and I can tell you their children's names and how long they have been married. I have a close bond with all these guys. I am really lucky—really lucky. Doesn't it sound fun? I'm pretty good at what I do, but it helps because you work with good people. You want to help them because they are good people. The one thing that I don't like is that I am so busy that I feel like I can't double-check myself. You want to read that e-mail a second time before you send it, but there isn't enough time to double-check, so that's my worst thing.

I feel like I've learned a lot. When I started here I was just a baby—I was just twenty years old—and now I can be a lot of these engineers' mom and almost their grandma, and so that's kind of cool too. I feel like I've just grown up here. I was raised Boeing. I'm more respected, and that makes me really happy. I feel like I've done a good job, and I feel like I have a really good life here at Boeing. I really do. I feel very happy. I think an office administrator has a totally different relationship with our management than engineers do; I get closer with people. Maybe not all office administrators are like that, but I'm that kind of person. I like to know who I am working with. I like to know not just how they work but how they are as people. That's how people respond to me, and it just seems to work out really good.

I had a wonderful manager. He had four daughters, and I was right in the middle of the [ages of the] two middle daughters, and I was with him for eleven years. So basically he raised me. We went through all the boyfriends and buying the first house and getting married and all that. He pretty much raised me. He was wonderful. And my engineers—I still keep in touch with some of them. I still keep in touch with these guys. I just love my job. I do. It's not just the work that I do but the people that I work with, that make it such a blessing to work here. Not everyone can say they've had a great boss or great people to work with. I've just been lucky. All the bosses that I've worked with have always been family first. If you need to leave—if something happens to your son—just do it. They are, "Just you take care of what you need to do," and that's always going to come first, and that's my opinion too. And so that makes me happy. Yeah, Boeing thinks like I do.

I am one of those people that if I'm upset, everybody knows it. I don't know if you can tell, but I'm not shy by any sense of the word, and I've slammed doors before, which was highly unprofessional. I'm a diabetic, so if I have low blood sugar I get a little more emotional than I should be. One day, I screamed and yelled and slammed a door, and my boss came in the room and just let me cry and put his arm around me and sat down by me. And asked what he could do to make it better. I couldn't believe it. One of my girlfriends said, "I can't believe how brave that man is, to go in and sit with you when he knew how mad you were." Oh my. But that only happens once in a while. Everything just came to a head, and it just happened when my blood sugar was low. So I got a little dramatic. Sometimes it just happens. It's just the way it is.

I just need two of me to get everything done, but they let me work as much overtime as I want. But then I run into not having a life outside. I've been married for a long time, and I have a sixteen-year-old son, so I go home pretty tired at night. I always tell my husband and my son that Boeing gets the best of me and they get the worst of me because I am so tired when I get home. But that's just the way it is. Nobody tells me I have to work this hard. Sometimes I wonder if I am just an idiot—I just give quite a bit.

I think they made some really poor choices, like what they did with the 787 when they decided to outsource almost everything, and then they realized that people that we outsourced to couldn't do what we do. I think rather than three or four years late—the 787 come out so late— we probably would have been a lot closer on time with our deliveries. But now we have delivered, and we have to go on. But I think it could have been a lot better if we would have never merged. When the McDonnell Douglas people came in, they brought in a different men- tality than the Heritage Boeing people. I think the management of Boeing has changed a lot since we merged with McDonnell Douglas, and I can't say it's all for the better. I just want to leave it at that. Yeah, it's upsetting. It really is. Not that any of them are bad people, it's just a different mentality than Heritage Boeing people seem to have, you know. I don't know, maybe I'd call it a different management style. Well, maybe I can't really wrap my hands exactly around what I want to say. I just don't feel as comfortable with those people. That sounds awful, but I just wish we wouldn't have done that—I wish we wouldn't have merged. I really do. Boeing is a really good place to work because if you are a good worker, they pretty much let you do what you need to do to be happy. At least they let me.

I say all this from the bottom of my heart: I have really only been blessed, I have been fortunate, I have worked with great people. I am very happy. I am just so happy. I still have a long time. I'm only fifty- two. I'm probably going to work—I'll have at least forty years in when I retire. I'm still just a kid. I still have a son to put through college. Yeah. I am really happy.

5

I WORK TO LIVE

One of the most obvious and common answers to the simple question "Why do you work?" often results in an equally straightforward answer: "To be paid." As noted earlier, Boeing has long enjoyed a reputation for providing the area's best pay and benefits to all of its employees—machinists, techs, engineers, managers, and office staff. Nearly everyone to whom we have spoken mentions this at some point as one of the advantages of working for Boeing. Compared to the alternative, Boeing is best. And yet, for some employees, this is *the* primary driver. Regardless of the company culture, corporate strategy, outsourcing, or behavior of top management, they return to the theme that they were well compensated when they began their employment and remain well compensated to this day.

Employees in this chapter are united by this common thread as they each emphasize how the company has provided good pay and benefits, which sustain them as they find and experience meaning outside work. The job provides good pay for them to support their families, take vacations, and purchase luxuries that they couldn't otherwise afford. Moreover, when they began their employment with the company, this was their modest expectation: anything above and beyond that basic arrangement has been a pleasant surprise. "When I came into Boeing, I didn't expect anything more than pay," commented one employee. And another remarked, "I think my expectations were met above what I had planned on. Never been to college to do what I do." As long as that basic exchange—good pay in return for a good day's work—has remained in place, they've chosen to continue their employment with the company. And as they wind down their long-term careers with the company, their original limited aspirations dip further. They may be fatigued from years of long work hours, unjust demotions, or changing technology, but they plan to "plug away" and perform their jobs well, retiring with satisfaction and pride for having given an honest "eight for eight" during their careers.

This is not to say, however, that work accomplishments or good coworker relationships are unimportant. Clearly, these make for a more enjoyable and satisfying work experience. One man speaks positively of the younger workers he is able to mentor, while another highlights the camaraderie among his workmates that makes day-to-day work life more enjoyable. Like employees featured in other chapters, these veteran employees are also sometimes critical of company decisions and corporate strategy, though these corporate actions seem to have had less impact on how they relate to the company or to their work. As one might anticipate, these employees conclude that younger workers, those who are newly hired to Boeing or just entering the workforce, can also find stable, well-compensated employment with the company. Boeing still offers that opportunity.

It is tempting to conclude that subscribing primarily to an instrumental exchange is good and sensible for both employees and organizations. Modest expectations on the part of workers are less likely to have the potential to disappoint, frustrate, or threaten a core identity. As such, these workers may be less resistant and more adaptable to fundamental corporate shifts. Having multiple ways to find meaning in life, such as family, religion, or even hobbies, is a less risky proposition as compared to making a strong emotional investment in organizations that make clear that they do not make emotional investments in their employees. And, importantly, these employees are proud of their work and report doing a good job. Yet we wonder if there is an unmeasured, silent cost associated with this more instrumental orientation—the cost associated with lost opportunity. Might it be the case for both employees and the company that the good has become the enemy of the great?

BEN LANDERS

If the kids' college finances were taken care of, I'd quit in a friggin' heartbeat. And it's not because I don't like what I do. I love what I do, and I love the people I work with. But I'm out of here. Fourteen years—5,300 and some days left. I just happened to calculate it.
—Program analyst and former manager, age fifty-two, twenty-five years at Boeing, interviewed in 2011 and 2012

I was attracted to Boeing because I'm actually a local boy. We moved from the East Coast to Washington in the summer of '67. My dad hired at Boeing and was laid off in 1970 with everyone else. I wanted to work for Boeing; didn't really care which position, just thought it was a cool employer, local, you know, big thing. When I came into Boeing I didn't expect anything more than pay. Anything's better than retail. I put on a shirt and a tie, work with people out in the factory, and I get a chance to deal with the airplane. I was in the 747 airplane daily, so that was pretty cool. I supported the final body joint area where they attach the wings and the fuselages together. I was in that area for probably two, three years and then moved to the wing body joint area. I joined the 777 program in 1989 and stayed for about fourteen years. I was an analyst and then a supervisor. I got busted out of management because of headcount reductions.

When you're in management, you're moving chess pieces. You're looking for the best resource to support that task. It's trying to develop your employees. I had a guy who came to me and said, "I like what I do, but this isn't what I want to do forever." And then it was my goal to help them get there. I could be, "Hey, that's great, but you don't have the skills to move on to that spot. So how can I steer assignments your way, to give you the skill, so it will build your resume to get you to that spot?" So when that happened, that was good. If it was a coach-y and counseling assignment where I could change my employees' behavior to make them better, that was good. When I let people go, if it was their own downfall, I'm okay with that. When I'm handing layoff notices to people, and through no fault of their own, they now have to look for a new job, that was painful. My wife says I'm a better person out of management than in management because I can leave the property.

I struggle with holding grudges. I worked for a senior manager who made the decision to bust me out of management when there were headcount reductions because of gender issues. Rather than be perceived as laying off the women, he sacrificed me and several other males. I had five second-level managers tell me that was what he was doing. Hey, equal opportunity laws? I don't believe that that was legal; nor do I believe that it was ethical. But at the time it was like, well, I didn't want to do that. Fear. I was newly married, with a child. I had responsibilities. Had I been single, no kids, I could have said, "Let's chat." If I get canned, then I get another job. So I ended up losing my management job. I figured if I ever win the lottery and figure out where that son-of-a-bitch lives, I'm going to buy a property on both sides of him and turn them into junkyards. It was painful because it was a real blow.

I'm proud of the company and proud of the things I work with. There are days when you come in to just get your work done, and satisfaction is with my wife and my kids because of what my job can provide for them. Other times, if I'm working on a project where I can see tangible results, that's always cool. There's always a better way to do something; if I can change a process for the good, then I feel a lot better. It drives my wife mad because I try to change stuff at home, and maybe that's not a good thing. I'm not in the airline, so I can't say, "Oh look, I designed that window or I designed a seat." I can't touch something tangible, but I can say, "Hey, I helped make sure we have the right resources where we need them to get the thing built. So everything came together the way it was supposed to." So I help try to save money, which helps the company get better products and maybe lower prices on airfares. If the kids' college finances were taken care of, I'd quit in a friggin' heartbeat. And it's not because I don't like what I do. I love what I do, and I love the people I work with. But I'm out of here. Fourteen years—5,300 and some days left. I just happened to calculate it.

We're seeing a lot of younger people come into industrial engineering. Two of them have PhDs. They were professors in the academic world, and then they wanted to work and learn firsthand, so they came to Boeing, which is cool. There are a lot of people who are in their twenties. I've got a T-shirt that's older than some of the people I work with, and that's okay because at some point, ya know, it's the passing of the baton. We try to guide them, to help them come up behind. There's a morale issue, and it's unfortunate because we have new people hiring in; there's a lot of people with Ns on their badges. The N indicates new employee; after three years the N goes away. We get a lot of good people that hire in. They come in as interns. They decide to come back to the company to work, and then once they get in, they see what appear to be bad decisions. It's like, "Well, where is this company going?" For a younger person, Boeing is the umbrella company, you might say, and it's what branch do you want to work in? I'm going to get my foot in the door, and I'm going into industrial engineering, but once I get in, then I'm going towards this or in that direction.

Personally, I'm okay with outsourcing to an extent. I believe that the company has some obligation to the employees as much as it has an obligation to the shareholders. The shareholders invest the money in the company. The employees invest time and effort. When you take work that is of a technical nature and move it to a Third World country that doesn't have that technology, that's a mistake. If you have an easy, very simple process that can be moved, for example, like insulation blankets, they could be moved anywhere around the world to someone who knows how to run a sewing machine. That's cool; I'm good with that. But if you're working with carbon fiber technology, there are very few places in the world that have the expertise and the knowledge for that. So I think outsourcing is good, but it has to be done quite judiciously as to what it is and where's it going. For example, I'm great with having Charleston, a production facility in the United States on the East Coast that is close to a port so you can bring parts in via ships as well as via air because they're next to an airport. It's work within the United States, which is good. Plus, honestly, I think the company needed to go into a right-to-work state, a state that isn't encumbered by the union. I'm okay with that too.

I'm not a big union fan, never have been. You know, the sad part is, I've seen union employees being defended by the union when the union representative goes, "I know this guy. He's a shit employee, he has crappy attendance, he's got a lousy attitude, he's got a poor work ethic, but as a union man, I have to defend him because he's been paying his union dues." That's bullshit. If you're a crap employee, get the hell off the property. I see too many union employees that hide behind the contract; they know their contract better than they know their own jobs.

So, yeah, I think going to Charleston was a good business decision. At some point there's going to be a frickin' bloodbath. This is just my opinion. I've only been here twenty-five years. I've seen strikes. I've seen builds and downs and builds and downs. Something tells me that at some point something is going to go splat. The company's going to look and say the '87 has to make money, and to do that they have to get rid of some of that labor overhead.

Different times of my career, I felt better about what I was doing. When I was affiliated with the 777 program, that was planned in my mind better. Things went better. Production, putting it through the flight-test program, and putting it in the hands of the customers all went more smoothly than what I'm doing with the 787 program. Now, we finally got airplanes delivered, and we're seeing airplanes moving, but we're years behind schedule. And this is the first time in my Boeing career I've been associated with a program that's sad. I'll say, "I'm on the 787 program. Yeah, we're losers. Yeah, it's a pretty cool airplane; yeah, I'm dying to fly on one as a passenger." But it's just embarrassing that we're this frigging far behind, and in my opinion it's because of the leadership and their decisions. We ask, "Why did you make the decision that you did?" I can only assume that on the mountain you're on, they've more information that I don't have, but just looking at what I've told ya, you've made a silly friggin' decision, and I don't understand why. It is frustrating—it really is.

When they merged with McDonnell Douglas, I thought that that was going to help strengthen and stabilize the company. We joke at work saying, ya know, McDonnell Douglas bought Boeing with Boeing's money. Their management style is different than what we were used to. We don't have leaders, we have managers. We had a leader: he went to Ford. I think that if we hadn't picked up McNerney, we would have been in better shape if we'd stuck with Mulally. Basically, they gave him the verbal finger when they picked McNerney. I found that if you don't know the products and services that your organization does, it's hard to manage it because people can pull your leg, and you're not smart enough to say, "Bullshit." So in the case of bringing a gentleman in from GE and losing a gentleman that had thirty-plus years in the industry who could say, "Bullshit," the 787 program would not have been in the woeful position that it is in currently. It's the spinners and

networkers who get promoted. A lot of them are just frickin' storytell-
ers. They can just spin yarn.

On anniversaries, you get a little pin that says five years, ten years,
whatever. You have a website you can look at, and it can give you
choices, and if you're at a certain year of service, you can order mer-
chandise. If you don't like the selection, you can translate that into
points if you want to buy something at the Boeing store, like a sweat-
shirt. The big swinger for twenty-five is you get an inside parking pass.
It takes ten minutes just to get to my car, and it takes another ten to get
off the property, so now, with my indoor parking pass, I get to park
closer to my building. Screw the twenty-five pin; I got an inside parking
pass. They also buy you lunch. Honestly, I could care less. I would
rather say, "Hey if you're going to take me to a fine restaurant, why
don't you just give me a gift certificate to that fine restaurant so I can
enjoy it with my wife?" So I had a fillet lunch; don't get me wrong, it
was a cool steak. But did they announce it at a staff meeting? No. They
gave me a formal congratulations and a hard handshake. It was like,
here's your service award; open it at your leisure. I ordered my watch.

I want to have positive memories. I try to keep a pretty good attitude. I show up every day. I'm a steady Eddie. I don't go out of my way
to make waves; I'm not going to kiss somebody's behind. I've been able
to work with people I enjoy working with. I would consider them work
friends, not friend friends. It's been a pretty good ride, but I hope
Boeing is going to stick around in the Puget Sound area. We'll see how
that goes. I've been pretty fortunate, and if someone wants to come into
the company, I would encourage them. And if they get laid off, don't
blame me. That's right. And I've only got fourteen more years to go.
Honestly, my dream job, once I retire, is to get a panel van and a
stainless steel cart; I want to drive the van to a park on a sunny day. I
want to wheel the cart down, tell some jokes, and I want to sell some
hot dogs. I imagine having a couple of hot dog stands like in *The Con-
federacy of Dunces*. That's my dream job, but I don't believe that would
support my kids in college, but if I'm retired, then it's that.

RICH KELLY

> I don't primarily get my self-worth from my job. [. . .] Our self-worth
> comes from God.
>   —Hourly worker, age sixty-two, thirty-three years at Boeing,
>   interviewed in November 2011

I started at Boeing in 1974. My wife and I had three boys at the time, the youngest being only three months old. We moved over here because I wanted to go to Bible College, but I also needed a job. My brother-in-law worked at Boeing and said his sister, who also worked there, could help me. I'd never met her—she wasn't part of personnel, but she worked closely with them. She told me to go down and apply for such-n-such job. I would've never thought that I had any skills that Boeing would want. So I hired in right on the bottom as a grade "0" and over the years moved up to higher-skilled jobs. I now work in a small area with several others and run various types of machines. It's something I never would've picked for myself, but I like it. I enjoy it because, like most guys, I like to be creative—to make things. I think it's a part of everybody's nature. If I can say it this way: Our Heavenly Father is the Creator, and he put his nature into us, giving each of us different talents and abilities.

Over the years things have gone up and down, but it's pretty much been a really good job. My wife's never had to work and—well, I won't say never. When the oldest two boys were around tenth grade and my younger son was in middle school and my daughter—she's a couple years younger than that—they were still both middle school age. So she taught Christian school for a year or two, the Accelerated Christian Education program. She did that for a couple years, while they were there; otherwise she's never really had to work because my job at Boeing has been sufficient. I enjoy going to work and supporting my family and allowing her to stay home with the kids.

There's been some major changes in recent years that I don't think have been good. The overall thing I see is that for years Boeing emphasized that people were their greatest commodity, resource, whatever, but that is not the message that is coming across now. And in fact, I wouldn't recommend anyone to go to work for Boeing right now. Now it might be totally different at other plants, but this makes me wonder about Boeing. . . . Cause it's been a wonderful job, but now people aren't being valued.

We had a boss come in, oh, I'm just going say twenty years ago—really sharp guy, an MIT grad, great people skills. He could take the worst employee and make them want to do their job and feel good about it. He'd let you know you mattered. I saw him work with the people that I knew didn't do their job. I mean, you could turn on your machine and just cut air for hours. You're not really producing anything. This boss would go up and talk to them and want to know, "Okay, what's the matter? How can I help?" This guy we've got now, he's several levels up, but he's the opposite. It's like the messages he gives is that people have no value, and he'd love to fire them. Even though it hasn't really affected me, I hate seeing people treated that way. It's not like there weren't some changes needed, but, see, this previous boss could've came in and made the changes, made everybody happy to change, and not take away from their value as an individual. This guy . . . totally opposite. I feel sorry for him. "You're making a mistake. What's the matter with you? Why'd you make a mistake? We don't make mistakes—mistakes cost us money." It's that type of thing. Be perfect and be faster; you're too slow. I don't respect him as a person. I respect his position, but I don't like the way he treats other people.

I don't primarily get my self-worth from my job. Yeah, sure, I like the fact that I have a good job, and I like doing it and always try to do a good job. But I don't really get my self-worth from that, but some guys do. I understand their thinking. I just think that their self-worth should come from a whole other area. In my way of seeing things, our self-worth comes from God. Each one of us is uniquely made by him, and our value and our worth comes from him. I love my Heavenly Father, and he loves me, and nothing can change that, even if I mess up. You want to do a good job for wherever you are—oh, absolutely, the scripture teaches that. Whatever you do, do it as unto the Lord. You know, doesn't matter if we are talking about Boeing or Microsoft. We're all the same!

PHIL LENS

> I'd like to be remembered as someone who gave Boeing 8 hours of
> work for 8 hours of pay. I really try.
> —Male quality assurance worker, age fifty-six, twenty-five years
> at Boeing, interviewed in February 2012

I know the first few years I was kind of bragging because it was such a
lifestyle change. I got about triple the amount of money than in construction. It showed, you know: I dressed nicer and started gaining
weight because I was eating regularly. I enjoyed what I did—the people
I worked with were sometimes a struggle—it took me about twenty
years until I started to get sort of bored with what I was doing. About six
or seven years ago was my twentieth-year period. And the last five or six
years, I've just counted the number of days until I can get out of there.
I'm getting to the age where I don't like surprises anymore, so when I
come in to work, I like to know what to expect. I'm the senior guy in my
group right now, so the guys come to me for advice, and I try to give my
wisdom. And the managers do as well. They come to us for expertise
because it's not their job to build parts but to manage. They're just
managing the people day to day. I like being in QA because there's a
certain amount of respect we get from the shop people; you can tell
them, "You can't do it this way." So it's nice having a little authority. I'm
pretty satisfied with where I've been. I thought about being a manager
for about a minute when I was a team leader. Then I thought about it
again later. A guy who did it regretted it the whole time. I talked to him
about it sometimes. Back then you got a crash course on people skills
and sent out to manage. In the meantime the people you worked alongside are giving you the biggest razzing: "Hey, you used to be one of us."
You put your Dockers on and go in every day, and they razz you about
that.

The overtime lately has been grueling. My whole life is suffering;
I'm getting to feel sort of exhausted. As far as having any fun, it's
tough—to have any time off. Whenever I do, I'm too pooped to do
much. So I rest instead of doing something fun. I'm hoping that it will
get a little better. They haven't made it mandatory yet, but there are
only several of us in our little group, so if I turn it down, the people with
less seniority than I will get the order to work, so I try to keep that
family feeling and work equal overtime. I could turn it down, but I take

my turn when it's time. There's a guy on second shift that has been on family leave with a sick wife, so he's taking a lot of time off, so we're filling in on second shift. It's like, "Aww geez." Hopefully she'll get well soon.

I've actually tried to help the kids of a couple people I know. They're smart kids. They're going to college and all that, and they're sharp. I told them, if you get the education, if there's an application, I'll help you fill it out. Once you're in the door, they'll train you for what you've got to do. And if you don't like it, you can request a transfer and do something else. I don't have any kids of my own, but I've suggested to quite a few other parents of kids who aren't satisfied and looking for something new. With the recession, Boeing has stayed solid. It's a little boring if you do the same thing for too long, but if you're young and energetic—I think that if you get your foot in the door, then you can try something else. I would suggest that to anybody. I have no regrets about working here; it's made it possible to do a lot of things, like vacations I wouldn't have gotten to do because of lack of money or having reliable transportation, and I'm just about ready to finish paying off my house.

I'm still kind of proud to say I work for Boeing, rather than at the dog pound or something. Compared to what I used to do, you know, people tend to treat you a little more seriously. If you're buying something and you say you're working in construction and you drive up in an old beater . . . if I'm looking at a new truck or something, they say, that guy won't be able to afford a new truck. He just wants a test drive. At least now they take you a little more seriously.

I'd like to be remembered as someone who gave Boeing eight hours of work for eight hours of pay. I really try. We in QA don't build the parts. We can only inspect what they give us, so sometimes there's a little sit-around time, but I try to find something to do. I try to give eight for eight whenever I can. I try to get along with as many people as I can and help people who are struggling. I'll probably never see it, but I hope that somewhere down the line that my advice would do somebody good. Help them advance or keep them from getting fired. I try to stay lighthearted. Try to smile easily. Try to help when they ask. I think my expectations have been met, above what I had planned on. I've never been to college to do what I do. Most places wouldn't even hire you if you didn't have college to do what I do, so I feel very fortunate to be where I'm at. I take pride that I'm doing something that not many people do. It's probably kept me where I'm at the longest; I'm pretty satisfied with my career.

I'm just looking to the end now, if I can just keep plugging away for the next few years. When I pick my date to retire, I'll start to count down. The only thing that's kind of holding me up is that I'm trying to get my ducks in a row first. My wife's elderly parents, she's taking care of them all the time. There's no use me retiring as long as she's still kind of chained to her folks, so I might as well stick around. Save up some more money. Get the house paid off. I have a lot of hobbies, so I keep my mind occupied at home. I started out doing a lot of woodworking. Now I've got a garage full of motorcycles I enjoy working on. I just got a new street bike before Christmas. That big bonus we got, I put it toward something I enjoy. Let the company pay for my bike.

6

PERMANENTLY SCARRED

Nothing can turn emotions as quickly or profoundly as betrayal. When trust and loyalty are violated, there is hurt along with anger and disenchantment. Something snaps and seems beyond repair. As Ken Hall says, after the merger, "everything changed." A subset of Boeing employees—once dedicated, engaged, and loyal—have become disengaged, disconnected, indifferent, and even bitter toward the company. Their antipathy for the postmerger company and its new business ethos is palpable and permanent.

From being proud to work for Boeing or thinking of it as "my company," they now either see it as a "paycheck" or "just another Fortune 500 company with no positive advantages." This change in their relationship with the company manifests itself in the way they approach their work. Ken Hall does a "good job," but he does not go "above and beyond anymore." Andrew Parks, once a lead engineer, now finds meaning in doing the work in the "right way" for the safety of the flying public. As for the company, he no longer gives "a hoot" and doesn't want to invest his time and energy in trying to change things for the better. He has no more goodwill left and is waiting to retire.

Our survey results show that about 10 to 20 percent of respondents manifest similar signs of alienation, as indicated in responses to statements measuring pride in the company, avoiding taking on extra duties, and feeling loyal to Boeing. More startling is that some 10 percent report working at 30 percent or under of their full potential—a heavy price in diminished work performance for the company. Clearly, these percentages describe a minority of Boeing's workforce, but their voices are important to hear. Besides reflecting an obvious psychological toll, these views comprise part of Boeing's present-day culture and, as such, have the power to affect and shape the perspectives of coworkers.

KEN HALL

> Yeah, I was kind of proud to work at Boeing and all, but that was earlier. You know, when I was younger and stupid, I guess.
> —Technician, age forty-eight, twenty-four years at Boeing,
> interviewed in 2011 and 2012

Everybody works for Boeing, at least, around here. My dad worked for Boeing. So I just tried that, and it worked. I had no specific desires at that time. Just to make a living and get by, I guess. And I've done that. There's no other work out there that pays as well—there's no other work right now. And basically, I make a good living. It's not that hard of a job. And it's comfortable for now. Kind of a deal.

I'm an electronics bench technician. In my area there'll be shelves that have to be tested: I go ahead and hook it up, and run the test, and fix the errors. My work doesn't make a difference because there are five or eight other testers for the exact same thing. If I'm not there, they keep right on going. It can be boring at times—the repetitiveness, the downtime. That's pretty much the worst part of it. I talk to other people, maybe see if I need training. I take my training, doing any kind of housekeeping, maintenance that I need to do. That's how I stay sane. My life is to have fun, and work is just a means to get there. So I'm not too dedicated to work, but I do a good job. You know. Going home, having fun. That's what I work for: being a father, being a husband, taking care of my family, enjoying my friends, just enjoying celebrations, parties, enjoying evenings on the deck. That keeps you going.

When you did your ten years, you got a diamond in your pin—a five-year pin, which is nothing—and ten years you get your diamond. Then it would go up. I think my dad got up to a ruby or an emerald. And then if you had fifty, you got a gold watch and a pin. Now you have to buy your stones and pins. I think at twenty-five years I got a watch. But they didn't even recognize me for a year and a half. It was like, "Whoops, we forgot about you." They'll call you for a handshake and a bottle of juice and "Good job. Now, go back to work."

I think McDonnell bought Boeing. Yeah, I can feel the difference. That's the way it looks, the way it feels. Everything changed. We were more of a family-type thing. You know, we felt more connected before-hand. We had parties outside work. We had Christmas parties. Not so much anymore. That's not only because of management. But it's also because people have gone their separate directions. Been laid off, taken other jobs, different positions. We're not a group anymore. It went from headquarters in Seattle to headquarters in Chicago. I became more distant, more disconnected to management, and to the job. Afterwards, the management looked at you as more of a number. I became a num-ber. I think that's pretty much when I stated just getting a paycheck. I think for a while I was pretty dedicated, and I probably went above and beyond, but now it's pretty equal. I don't go above and beyond any-more. When we were more of a family, I would help my family out. Now, it's not a family, so I don't help. Before that, we had fun. Now we don't have fun, we just work. To me it's a job, and it's a good-paying job.

Well, the management, it seems to be more of an attitude to where they want to make more money. They don't really care how it's done; everything is based on a "Let's make sure this job gets out on time. I don't really care if it's right or not—just get it out on time." There's a lot more pressure to get things out on time. They say quality is the main concern and all that, but they don't act that way. They value the bottom line. Can I build it cheaper? Boeing lost their identity when they merged. Now it's . . . who knows what it is? Basically what any company stands for: make a buck.

I don't really trust management a whole lot, and I don't really get a whole lot of job satisfaction out of being disappointed in things. The name of the company is going away. Yeah, I was kind of proud to work at Boeing, but that was earlier. You know, when I was younger and stupid, I guess. The 787 is one of the huge disappointments; not being able to deliver quality is a disappointment. They're three years late on the 787. People who are newer to the business—newer to the process and not actually there putting the wings on—they may not care as much about their process. What they care about is whether or not they get a paycheck. It is a [daily problem]: that's why we have airplanes sitting out on the tarmac right now with jobs that aren't complete. That's why we're three years behind. I'm embarrassed that the project was so late and behind schedule. One of the problems that we have is we spend a lot of time reworking the parts to make them fit. You're dealing with cultural differences, communication differences—they don't really care as much about the airplane. The airplane builders, the people who are there right now in Everett, they care a lot about their jobs. What effect is the lower quality going to have on the Boeing name? Are the customers going to be as committed to a Boeing product if it's inferior? It's gone beyond, you know, the normal problems that you have with a new program. Boeing promised a product, and they're standing behind that product, but yet, that product is not . . . it doesn't contain the quality, and it's a little more inferior than what I would expect out of Boeing. It's not what I would expect of the Boeing that I grew up with. It wouldn't happen with Boeing of yesteryear.

Yeah, I'm in a union. And that's it. That's all I can really say about it. I don't like the union. I haven't been a member for quite a while because being in a union, to me, is being a sheep. It's just doing what they want. The union leaders aren't looking out for our best interests. They're looking out for their own. I would rather make my own decisions and not have someone else make the decisions for me. We went on strike a while ago. I hate going on strike. But I don't have any real effect on whether or not I go. It's a group decision. And I was thinking of crossing the line because my family was shorted. I wasn't making any money. They called me at my home, and they threatened my family. I was threatened. My family was threatened before I did anything, so that pretty much sealed the deal there. So I don't think that's a very good position for them to take. That happened once, and now I won't answer the phone. I wish that the company was trustworthy enough to not need a union.

So I just work for a while until I'm done. I need to get my house paid off. At fifty-nine to fifty-nine-and-a-half you can retire without penalty. Fifteen years maybe? Get my house paid off—that's ten years from now. Ten years is a long time. Who knows what will happen between now and then?

ANDREW PARKS

> I used to be a Boeing engineer; now I am an engineer that works at
> Boeing. That is a very difficult paradigm shift.
> —Engineer, age forty-seven, over twenty years at Boeing,
> interviewed in 2011

I began my career in the late 1980s, working on a defense project. The technically interesting projects, particularly the International Space Station, drew me to Boeing over the other companies which offered positions to me. I knew Boeing was the prime integrator or system provider on most projects, rather than a supplier or subtier contractor. I felt working from the top of the integration pyramid would give me broad insights into all aspects of a project rather than a more limited viewpoint, which would come from working at an equipment supplier or a lower-level integrator.

High points [of my career] were being appointed lead engineer, being recognized as a designated engineering representative of the FAA, and successful completion of a couple of challenging projects and the engineers strike. Low points were (1) receiving a WARN notice two years after joining the company, only to learn that my position was given to a friend of my manager for a period of three months while they waited for their retirement date; (2) the realization that senior management was much like our congresspersons in DC—much more interested in their careers than in serving the company; and (3) witnessing clearly unethical and immoral behavior of middle managers and recognizing that the culture not only allowed but promoted such.

I wasted seven years of my life on that [787] program. I'm not proud of that airplane or how we got that to fly. I think it's a safe product, but I think it's a bad example of how to do an airplane program. And I'm particularly ashamed of that program because of what I think is blatantly dishonest communications to the public and our investors about how the program was going in terms of hiding known problems, hiding the extent of problems, and just outright lying about the progress of the program. I've moved to a different program which is earlier on in its development phase, so pressure's off in terms of performance, but I hear the same kind of things. I think it's a little better in my particular corner of the world now from the program management level. But from the corporate management level, I don't see much change in their tone.

I think middle managers have learned lessons, and they were ground kind of beneath the steamroller too. I've seen a lot of refugees that have fled to other programs and kind of licking their wounds at the same time, so the middle managers seem to be more sensitive to those sorts of issues.

The local management has gotten a little bit better; they're more responsive and more open to ideas—that has gotten better. And they're more welcoming. The reason I bring it up is some of the same managers that were bad actors on the 787 are not so bad off the 787. Most of the coworkers I work with now are refugees from the 787 and are taking jobs that are less stressful, less demanding, and less pressure filled. I hear them talking about the 787 virus spreading, noticing the 787 mentality creep in, but I would say that they all expressed to me their stress level and work overload is less.

Since 2006 there's been an increase in antiemployee sentiments among corporate managers. There's been an increase in pessimism regarding corporate management among the employees, and there's been, I think, a worker decline in loyalty toward the company. I would say that attitude has been demonstrated by the corporate leaders to their workforce and how they meet programs, how they view employees as a resource to be used without regard to the employee's well-being, despite what they say—massive overtime, unrealistic deadlines, understaffing, unrealistic expectations toward work attitude.

We'll never know for sure what lessons they learned from things like the 787 and other programs that are run similarly. Whatever they learn, I hope they communicate the fact that I've learned it, and here's the lesson we learned, and here's what we're doing differently. We just don't hear a lot of communication so that leaves us without a lot to grasp onto in terms of "Are we making the right progress or not?"

I think outsourcing is a valid concept, but I think that as with all things, theory is much different than reality. The examples I have personal experience with have been disastrous. I've dealt with a Moscow design center project where they offloaded, you know, Boeing work to a Boeing design center made up of people they cobbled together and reduced Boeing staffing accordingly, right? You end up spending five times as much, literally, fixing their errors, explaining, communicating, just finally doing their work for them. Management has told us, and I'm speaking just a few years ago, "We don't want to hear your whining about how much rework you," I'm quoting them, "we don't want to hear your whining about how much rework you have to do. Just get it all done." That's a direct quote from a senior executive manager. So outsourcing is an appropriate strategy if they do it properly and ethically. I'm not sure in cases I've directly experienced they've properly done it.

[Regarding the second assembly 787 line in South Carolina,] I don't really have any feelings about that. I think it's a good business decision to have redundancy. You know, you've heard about companies that got wiped out by a tornado, then, oops, there goes the company, so I think in terms of business capacities it's a smart decision. Whether it was fair to the people and what promises they made to the machinists and then went back on, I don't know anything about.

I'm a member of the engineering union, the SPEEA union. It became mandatory, I don't know, fifteen years ago, something like that. I was a member before then, so pretty much my whole career. I think Boeing feels like it has leverage over the unions, so is being a bit nicer about it but still giving them the screw. Boeing would be happy if there were no unions. I think it's a matter of chasing the average, right? We have to do it because the rest of America's doing it, so we have to have co-pays on our insurance because the rest of America is, but everyone's saying that, so who's leading the charge there? It's like rents for apartments, right? You go with the market rate because everyone else is charging that. I think, as goes America, so goes Boeing. Eventually the unions will lose some of their bargaining power.

I used to be a Boeing engineer; now I am an engineer that works at Boeing. That is a very difficult paradigm shift. I was grateful to Boeing for the chance to create a career in an enterprise which offered so many great projects and opportunities and decided early on that I would give my entire career to Boeing. I decided long ago to retire from Boeing, along the lines of how a Japanese worker would dedicate a career to a company. I was my company, my team, and its success was my success. That was a prime motivation until the events that led to the engineers' strike. After the strike, my motivation was that my work was important to the flying public and that doing the right job, the right way, was one prime source of meaning in my job.

You know, I'm past the point of caring about the company frankly. I used to recommend Boeing as a preferred place to work to friends and colleagues—even recruiting a couple—and would have done so for my children. However, now to me Boeing is just another Fortune 500 company with no positive advantages. I retire in a few years, so I really don't give a hoot, and I wouldn't waste my time making input because I would never see fruition. I just don't want to invest my time or energy into that anymore. I spent my whole career trying to change the company, and I used up all my goodwill. No more left. So I haven't been spending time thinking how to make it better, which is kind of a sad thing. Suck it up and get the job done. You can only do that for so long though. I cope with it intellectually. I understand where it comes from. I compartmentalize it. It's just a physical fatigue and reduced energy that you can't really escape. Mentally I can divorce myself from the job pretty much. You know, stress is a bad thing for aging. The work overload kills sleep, so in combination it really decreases the energy you have, your emotional resilience, most of your energy levels, and your tolerance to frustration. Yeah, my health has declined. I've aged probably double the normal rate in the last five years on the 787 program. Much to my regret I used to sacrifice family time to support projects and programs. Now I give the company my best effort within bounds of availability and have distanced myself from the company's success or failure on given projects.

7

ATTACHED TO WORK, DETACHED FROM COMPANY

The three employees in this chapter illustrate a number of themes we have often heard as people have told us about their reactions to the company's new direction and culture. These are common motifs, illustrating frequent frustrations, concerns, and coping styles among long-time employees. Much like those in the previous chapter, employees in this chapter express a great deal of criticism of company leaders, their decisions, and Boeing's overall corporate philosophy since the merger with McDonnell Douglas. This is especially demonstrated by the reactions to the company's decision to outsource so much of the 787's design and manufacturing work. Although employees may say that they're not necessarily opposed to the outsourcing concept, they point to example after example of 787 problems stemming from incompetent production, to layers of subcontracting, and to poor oversight of the process. To be sure, criticism of the company's top leadership and new corporate ethos is found among employees outside this chapter too. The remarks here, however, reflect a fairly complete condemnation, with interviewees failing to find any positive angle to this new company strategy and identity.

More broadly, we hear from these employees much concern for the company's and even the country's broader economic fate. They worry that the current leadership is driving the company into the ground or that corporations today fail to support the broader US economy in a way that will sustain the average American worker's lifestyle. Concern for the future, however, is not limited to the decisions made by top management. Employees in this chapter also express the view that the new generation of workers coming to Boeing are not being well trained, are not as emotionally invested in their work, are not as committed to working hard, and do not understand the need for union protection and support. Indeed, these interviewees harbor a certain cynicism and hopelessness toward this new generation of employees that matches the cynicism and hopelessness they direct toward the company as a whole.

Given such concerns about the future and their mistrust of company leadership, it is perhaps not surprising that employees in this chapter are all supporters of the union, believing that the power of the group is needed to protect the pay, benefits, and safety of employees. These views are generally not representative of the broader workforce, yet reflect a significant perspective we include here. From our survey data from International Association of Machinists and Aerospace Workers (IAM) and Society of Professional Engineering Employees in Aerospace (SPEEA) members, we note that positive attitudes toward unions' current effectiveness range from roughly 30 percent for areas such as "reducing outsourcing" and "improving workplace productivity" to 85 percent for issues like working conditions, pay, and benefits. General employee reaction toward union effectiveness in the future, however, is low: only some 10 percent of employees believe that unions will be very successful in the future, even when bargaining for the historically important bread-and-butter issues. Nonetheless, the positive views from employees in this chapter represent an important theme for a subset of veteran employees.

Last, despite their strong, negative judgments toward Boeing, their disengagement from the company, and even their disconnection from the outsourced products, these interviewees each, somewhat remarkably, remain deeply connected to their day-to-day work. This commitment is narrow and specific: they are invested in their work tasks, their professions, or working with others to solve problems. They seem able to contend with their high degree of negativity and pessimism about the company and its future by delving into the specifics of their work and remaining dedicated to high-quality performance.

It is difficult to gauge the impact of this reaction. On the face of it, one could argue that both the company and the individual benefit in terms of strong work engagement, satisfaction from a job well done, and high-quality work performance. But, as in other chapters, we wonder whether such an approach results in hard-to-perceive costs linked to poor morale or low company regard.

JAMES MORRIS

> Engineers get to make the airplanes; we get to go against the Airbus engineers. Mano a mano. It's my engineers against your engineers. I like the competition; the company doesn't.
> —Engineer, age fifty-nine, thirty-three years at Boeing, interviewed in 2012

My dad was an engineer, and my mother was a teacher, so I grew up with problem-solving attitudes. I was going to college during the Boeing bust years—the supersonic transport days, when the company almost went out of business. I kind of floundered a little bit before I finally realized my mentality as an engineer. I'll get an engineering degree and then figure out what I want to do. I got offers from three companies. An Arizona company blew it on the day of the interview. They took me back to HR, laid out a roadmap of the state of Arizona, and said, "You want to do some sea fishing? Two and half hours to go down here. You want to go skiing? Two hours. You want to go hiking? Two hours." One of the other options was here at Boeing in metal development. Okay, I'm from Puget Sound, thirty minutes to the ski slopes, twenty minutes to the salt water. I chose Boeing because of the weather and the girl-friend. All three jobs were challenging, and not to give my wife a swelled head, but I chose her.

My degree is in metallurgical engineering. When I went in, the bearings were basically World War II bearings with seals. As a metallur-gist I went in and tweaked the alloy, changed the carbon content, changed the silica or the selenium content, asked, "What is this going to do?" Developed a new alloy, asked, "What properties am I aiming for? Corrosion? Crack resistant? Strength?" So you tailor the alloy for what you want. Nowadays the metals I'm using are more aligned for higher strength. We've improved the seals, we've improved the grease, and we have improved the metals, so in a lot of cases I've gone one or two generations. At the beginning you got help, but mostly you are trying to figure things out yourself. I went in and grabbed a big chunk. Some people do. I'd say the majority of people in engineering thrive in that environment. Some don't, and they disappear. They go elsewhere or leave the company.

I'm past retirement age at Boeing, but I don't walk out and leave things as they are. I could, but these people need to learn the job so they can continue my job afterwards. Most engineers are very much that way. We consider ourselves professionals. Right or wrong, we have a professional job. For example, in layoffs, one of Boeing's first rules is to move the employee away from that job where they could do damage when they give the person the sixty-day notice of possible layoff. They do that on the shop floor, and they tried the same thing with the engineers. We are engineers, extremely professional—not to say the shop isn't, but we take pride in our work cause this is not an airplane, this is our baby. So we want to shepherd it through. We convinced Boeing not to withdraw the engineers from the workplace, which they reluctantly agreed to. They came back at the end of the sixty days and laid off some people, but they had to drag those engineers out as they were still trying to do their jobs.

Engineers get to make the airplanes; we get to go against the Airbus engineers, mano a mano. It's my engineers against your engineers. I like the competition; the company doesn't. When Boeing pretty much took over the market for airplanes from Douglas and Lockheed, they were very arrogant. Then we were competing with Airbus, our design against their design. We have different philosophies. Boeing came from building the best aircrafts, the Cadillacs where they were very fault tolerant—keep on beating, keep on ticking. Airbus went a different route, to lower cost. A few years ago Boeing decided that they only had to be good enough; they didn't have to be number one. They were quite willing to make a better profit and be number two, whereas engineers want to tweak things. There is a point where you have to take the job away from engineering and start production because every engineer can go back and just make that a little bit better. I don't know if you want to call it ego or professionalism.

The average age of the engineers is about fifty-four years old. In the past Boeing went through boom-and-bust cycles, buildups and layoffs, buildups and layoffs. When I joined, I was part of the leading wave of fresh people, but then they go and virtually hire nobody younger for ten years. So you've got this wave approaching [age] sixty; then you have a dearth of people followed by a secondary wave ten to fifteen years younger. You got some spotting in between, but there is a problem. Boeing doesn't understand how long it takes to make someone very effective. It took one of our other engineers seven years. Part of it is that I don't see the long view in the young workers that are coming in. I see just a short-term solution. You know, they're trying to accomplish this one task, whereas I'm trying to teach them to look ten, fifteen years down the line. What's going to be happening? What adjustments do you need to make in this design?

SPEEA is very effective for its members on many levels. Where SPEEA's having troubles along with everybody else is how to engage the younger members. Everywhere, you see across the United States, when you get to younger workers in the workforce, those in their twenties up to midthirties as a broad brush, a lot of them don't see a total future with the company. So they don't engage on many levels: they do their job and are ready to move on to something else. They're not into putting the effort in for your fellow workers.

The merger with McDonnell Douglas in the nineties changed the culture of Boeing; the McDonnell Douglas management brought in the "kill or be killed" environment. Though there's less working together than there used to be, the main goal of SPEEA and the IAM is to make the company survive. But the union's side goal is also to help share some of the wins when the company's workers produce profits, just like the shareholders. Unions think workers should be recognized and rewarded with more of a risk sharing. The companies look at it as wages versus just good enough. If I can go to China and have it made just good enough, then it's only profits. They're not interested as much today in the US workforce. I think the company should be more interested in America. Some of the jobs that were outsourced are coming back. Even Starbucks is investing in the United States, putting US-made cups in the shops for sale, rather than just made in China. That's what a US company should be concerned about. Not just the bottom line, because who's your future customers? The airlines are filled with US citizens flying across this country; they have to have a decent job to be able to afford that. That was invented by Henry Ford. He paid his workers well so they could afford to buy a car from him. I would much rather see both sides working together. Both need each other. You make money by manufacturing things. Bringing manufacturing to other countries leaves the United States very vulnerable. It becomes more of a service industry. You can't make much at McDonald's.

As a union we are different than most unions. First, you have a bunch of crazy engineers in it. We went on strike a number of years ago against Boeing. It was not over money; it was not over benefits; it was that we wanted respect. The company had just turned us into numbers, and so the engineers, who are definitely not just in it for the money, actually went on strike, which surprised a lot of people, including Boeing. And some of us, some of the union people, were dumbfounded by it also. I was very proud of the engineers who were willing to do this. It was basically the first strike of that type in our nation's history.

For the most part engineers don't have a union-type mentality. They all think they can negotiate better deals with their bosses. Yeah sure. You really can't. The companies have always got the advantage over the employee. The only way you can counter that is forming a cooperative party, which is typically a union [that is] able to negotiate those benefits. My experience has shown over the years that companies will seesaw back and forth. There are companies out there who are still good to their employees; employees won't form a union. In a good company workers don't feel the need, because the company represents them adequately.

Most of the application I've seen on outsourcing has been to the detriment of the company. Initially, we would only outsource to somebody who knows the product better than we do. Most of the time now the outsourcing has been to companies who don't know what they're doing. But I guess the price is right. Spirit builds the fuselages for the 737 and some of the cabs, and they ship it up to Puget Sound to have the wings put on and the interior. On the 787 program, we outsourced the wings to Mitsubishi Heavy Industries. We built the tooling and all the technology in Seattle, built something like the first seven sets of wings, then turned it over to Mitsubishi to continue making. That was not outsourcing to somebody who knows the product better. In South Carolina we ended up buying Vought, so that now Boeing owns the plant because they were not putting good-quality products out. The parts from Italy are just really below grade; in Italian there's really no word equivalent of "shall"; everything is optional. Chinese parts are improving, but that also involves trying to get around culture problems. For example, the quality assurance in China has been that if you turn in something for bad work, the worker loses money, and it's punishing the families. I'm seeing inferior steel that doesn't meet spec; they don't have the technical know-how, and they're still in an agrarian type of environment that they've grown up in. The company tried to go off in a new direction without adequate foresight, ignoring the voices from below and only hearing the voices from above. Engineering told them— many people did—that they were cutting off too much in trying to totally outsource everything, but they continued on because they'd already made a decision.

As an engineer, I like multiple redundancy; I use it for buying parts. I want multiple sources to prevent an act like earthquakes or something else disrupting production. It's how it was done that I disagree with. We had people from the fuels and lubricants group who went to South Carolina to help them solve a problem, and they're put into a different building and isolated so they would not contaminate the workers in South Carolina. There's the undocumented process where I guess the loyalty of the employee is checked. Names are supposed to be sent to a certain manager in South Carolina for review prior to designating the people. The people are reviewed. I don't know how they think they can hinder knowledge of wages and anything else, but that seems to be the intent.

The first rollout of the 787 was a lot of smoke and mirrors. Landing gear didn't match. What is this plastic doing on the wings? Those doors look funny. Turns out they are held in place by 2 × 4s. That's why it took three years from rollout for the airplane. It wasn't ready. But because of the date and the 787 airplane number, the airplane had to roll out the door on July 8, 2007. They rolled it out and rolled it back in. Boeing's fiasco on the 787 was so bad that even upper management noticed. Originally outsourcing for the 787 was, in theory, to get other companies to do the investment; everybody makes a profit. The 787 was so poorly conceived and implemented that it has cost us two to three times what it would have cost to build in house.

I'll probably retire in three years. When I do retire, I've got to have something to do, whether it be Boeing or an experimental aircraft club or something, I've got to find something to do with my mind. There are retirees that still work with SPEEA after they retire. A lot of engineers come back as contractors; it gives them something to do part of the year. But I'm not ready to retire. Yes, you remember some of the negatives, but they don't seem so negative, and after a while, you re-member your successes—new alloys, new bearings. I've helped people my whole life, so I see people all the time that I helped make a change or something sometime in the past. Everybody you touch, you affect. I can see a lot of people I've helped. When I die, there will always be some things unfinished. I won't be in the history books, but a lot of people have better lives or careers or enjoyment from things I've helped them with. I can walk with pride. Will it mean anything to anybody? To me, yes. Did I dedicate too much time to the company? Yes. But it's something I wanted to do, something you don't necessarily get paid for. There is a sense of satisfaction with that. And I'm not done yet. I feel sorry for the nursing home.

JOHN LORIE

> Because of the loss of pride in the company, because if you think, "Oh, I'm just a number here, I'm here just to get paid. I'm doing my job. I put in my eight hours." [. . .] Sure, that attitude can certainly be there. If it dominates you, that's another question. It hasn't dominat-ed me.
>
> —Sheet metal worker, age sixty, twenty-eight years at Boeing, interviewed in 2011

I started in Boeing in 1980. Boeing was hiring at that time to build the 767 and 757 airplanes. Finished the work there at Green River and they hired me out of the class—hired the whole class. There were sixteen of us. They put us into an experimental shop, so we were the ones to build the very first parts of both of these planes. We all initially worked together. Loved it. Loved it. Loved it. I'm one of the last of that group where Boeing was still hiring but you didn't have to have a degree. I'm a big pusher for kids in school, the trade schools. We need trade schools bad. To push college as the only [path to] success—you know? It's nuts.

I've enjoyed my job. We built many different things, and I've gotten to know people in different labs because sometimes we have to visit those labs to set up something for them that we've built. Seeing what they're testing and stuff, we get to have that personal relationship with the lab folk. I've enjoyed that very much. And then just fellow mechan-ics, we all have different talents; we all have different skills. We have friendships that have developed over the years, mainly at work. We'll even have a little social at work, like for a break or lunch, or we'll have a little snack for somebody's birthday or something. Not all groups do that, that's for sure—we're fairly close. Oh, we tease each other and have fun with each other. We can yell at each other or laugh at each other. We've got all the emotions. We're human (laughs).

This job at Boeing sort of came to me. It was like a gift to me—that's how I take it. I could have gone this road or this road; well, I went this road. And why that happened, fate, you know, or you have a God looking over you, or what, you know. But I want to give credit where credit is due. And I'm not always the master of my life, you know. There's other things that are happening out there in the world . . . in the spiritual world . . . that we're guided, and so I think that deserves a lot of credit there. And I was listening. I had enough sense to listen, you know. And so I went that route.

I think that the culture of Boeing has changed since we bought McDonnell Douglas. We bought McDonnell Douglas, but unfortunately the Boeing Company had to absorb a bunch of their management people. Because of their management people, their process was very different than the Boeing process at the time—the business process. And so I think that drug us down. I think that was, like, the beginning of a lot of the problems that we have now. We should have never agreed to absorb their upper management, like their chief executive officer, Stonecipher, and stuff like that.

In '95 or '96, I don't remember the years, but there was a lot of turmoil going on. Condit was head of our company then, and we went from the family-type feeling thing. I know it's a cliché to say that, but, you know, people felt very proud of working for the Boeing Company, and we put out a very good product. We put it out on time, within budget, and we were very proud of that, a very safe product, you know, so safety is huge. But then Condit sort of changed that. Once he started that process, we just sort of became a number, and that's a cliché statement. But we instantly, within our hearts, we instantly changed our attitude towards the company. We felt that the top leadership that was going to be put in place after this merger was mostly the poor quality of the management of McDonnell Douglas instead of our own Boeing people that are tried and true. And so then, sure enough, that's what they did, and we've made some horrible mistakes. Their commercial side of McDonnell Douglas was really a flop at the end there, and yet we brought that man in—the very top guy from McDonnell Douglas, he came in and led Boeing.

We lost a lot of pride in our company once that happened, and it hasn't rebounded like it should because of these huge mistakes that they're making now under McNerney. When he was brought in, we were already on a downward slide with Stonecipher from McDonnell Douglas, and then McNerney is the captain. He always makes it look good, you know, that the company is making a profit, because of the traditional huge retirement packages and bonuses that they get. And everyone on the board, of course, is getting a bonus as well. That's a terrible way to run a company. It's almost a hundred-year-old company. It will be in 2016; the last decade has been very poorly managed.

And some of these [top management decisions] are such large gross errors that you just wonder, how do they even have a job? How do they keep getting their huge retirement bonuses? They never get stopped, fired. When's the last time you ever heard of anybody in the top management of Boeing being fired? They let Condit go, and they let Stonecipher go, [but] it wasn't because of their business plan. It was because they were caught with women. It was the embarrassment to Boeing that their top people were, you know, being involved. It wasn't because of what they were deciding at the boardroom and how to run the company, and that's what needs to change.

So I appreciate the company, it's a great company to work for, but I think under this new management, the top management subcontracting things out . . . they made foolish mistakes, and it's cost us. For example, now with the 787, which was an outrageous sum at the time, we figured it somewhere between $10 and $12 billion to develop this new 787. Well, they've subcontracted this plane out, a lot of it—80 percent or whatever the figure is—around the world. Some of those companies have never built or dealt with these kinds of specifications, and we've had to yank their programs from them. Italy is a prime example, and South Carolina was a big mess. I think that there was absolutely no doubt that Boeing wanted to punish the current workers out here in Seattle, the Puget Sound area. It doesn't make sense for some of the parts that have been made around the world, to ship them all the way to South Carolina. It was something that they thought that they could save a bunch of labor costs, and we'll see. They deliberately chose a right-to-work state for this. Again, another business plan mistake.

And so now the development of that 787, instead of costing $10 to $12 billion, went up to $16 billion, went up to $20 billion, and now it's in the low $30 billion to develop one plane. That could, like, bankrupt your company. Three and a half years late! Ridiculous. Just absolutely ridiculous. But this was their grand experiment. Well, we—me as an IAM member of the local union—we tried to tell them with our experience, "You can't be doing this." You can subcontract out certain things, but there's certain things that you never want to subcontract out. Like, for example, the wings. Well, that all went to Japan. So that's the first time ever in Boeing's history that we ever farmed out our wings, which is a major thing in the airplane. We're holding our breath that none of them fall out of the sky. If one of those crashes, God forbid, then it's grossly embarrassing for us as well as grossly embarrassing for the top management and the board.

Anyway, we thought it was foolish, and we've seen now what has happened over these years and the extra cost. They're going to have to deliver over 1,000 of these 787s to make a profit now instead of 250 or 300 airplanes to make a profit. But yet this guy still has a job; he qualified for his $40 million pension plan—just his pension plan! They get all these perks even though they're slowly, almost deliberately driving the company into the ground. That's my personal opinion (laughs). I'm seeing this in a lot of different companies across America, so I'm wondering, "What are these professors teaching at the college level? Why are these corporate guys all doing the same things?" I think it boils down to greed, you know. They are greedy people, and they can't admit that they're making mistakes. Their egos won't allow them to, and it's a very sad thing for American companies. You can talk until you're blue in the face, but until decisions are made to change the system, there's nothing you can do; you have to work within the system. Well, you just give up.

In the Puget Sound area I think it [the future of unions] is strong because people know—they have a sense even if they're new—that without the union, there would be less wages. They can't negotiate for themselves. At least anyone that has a brain. . . . South Carolina is going to have to learn that the hard way. They're eventually going to learn it— I think eventually they will go union. Right now they're just glad to have

a job. The company is going to deliberately keep their wages and benefits as low as possible. And that's the company's goal, that's the purpose
of them moving there. They're going to be paying those people at $15
an hour back there; out here the same people would be getting $20, $25
an hour. The new hires have no history of what we have been fighting
for all these years and trying to maintain—you know, pension, medical,
that type of thing, medical for the retirees. They have no sense of that
because they don't know the history of what we've been fighting for
over the last thirty years.

Because of the loss of pride in the company, because if you think,
"Oh, I'm just a number here, I'm here just to get paid. I'm doing my
job. I put in my eight hours. I'm working overtime if overtime's available, I got things in my personal finances that I want to accomplish,"
sure, that attitude can certainly be there. If it dominates you, that's
another question. It hasn't dominated me. You still have a product to
put out; you still should have some pride in your product. So if somebody asked me, "Do you work for Boeing?" I'd say, "Yes, I work for
Boeing." I haven't lost all pride in the company, of course not. I've
enjoyed the wages and the benefits that I've gotten over the years. I'm
glad of what I have done for the company and glad that I've been able
to stay there for at least twenty-eight and a half years. I'm glad that I'm
looking forward to retirement with a decent retirement. That has all
been a plus for me, for my life, for my family. I've tried to encourage my
nieces and nephews to get on at Boeing, especially now—a number of
them have lost their jobs, but for some reason nobody's taken my advice.

I'm going to ride this out until I decide to retire, and that's coming
up in probably three years. The only thing that would affect me is if the
Boeing Company tried to sub out all of the flight tests for testing brand-
new airplanes. You need to keep that in house. That was one of the
issues that we had to fight with the union. It was a very dangerous move
for the company to rely on other companies to flight-test their planes
and then believe in those results, you know. Again it's *the* very top
management making those kinds of foolish decisions that just scares the
hell out of us here on the floor. I have no trust in management whatsoever. Rather than survivorship of our product and our company, our
top management—they're thinking more global. I think it's very dan-

gerous. We're going to lose quality over that, and they're eventually going to lose control of the company.

JOE RICARD

> The relationships you have with people within the company is incredible, you know, and you meet up with people, just out of the blue, you'll work a project with somebody. The synergy's right there, and that's the cool part about it. That's what makes it what it is . . . just solving problems, just being the guy without the four-year degree that can look at something and go, "Gosh, why don't you try that?" . . . Bing. There it was. So it was like the coolest thing, you know.
>
> —Mechanic, age forty-eight, twenty-five years at Boeing, interviewed in 2012

I came into Boeing as a mechanic, but they put me in machining because I hired six months before they really needed mechanics, so the placement was horrible. I applied for a mechanic's job, got a mechanic's job, walked in the door. I said, "So where's the airplanes at?" "What airplanes? What do you mean airplanes? You're making parts. Get over there, get to work." Horrible place. Dirty. Nasty. Loud. You know, just no fun. You get a stack of parts—you know, bend them, drill them. They call it part fabrication. That's all you did: stamp, bend them, straighten them. They come out of the heat treat ovens; they'd be all crooked, you put them on a table, you bend them flat. Yeah, it was driving me crazy—I hated it. And so I said, "Well, they offer education—I'll go to school at night. Eventually I'll have enough education that I can go anywhere." And that's what I did. I started going to school four nights a week, and then an offer came up in Developmental.

During this time I volunteered to work on disassembling a wing. And the wing happened to be in an area that the research guys were going to move into. There's three guys in that clique; they weren't getting the job done, and this manager knew he could count on me, so he came to me and says, "Hey, I need to take this wing apart." So whatever, you know, I'll do it. It was hard. You had to climb inside this thing and cut out a piece of material—it was after they tested the wing, so there was a cracked piece inside; you had to get that out so they could look at it under a microscope and study it. Just nasty in there. It was no fun. But I did it, you know. "Well, you're union, you know, you shouldn't do it." "No, I don't care, whatever you need, I'll do it, you know." And so, pretty soon I started doing all this stuff for these guys, and they said, "Well, we'd like you to stay here with us."

I took on a position of responsibility to get what they need to do the development work. And I love it because it's my own little group. We have what are called techs, technicians, that work with the engineers also, but I'm a true salted mechanic. I've got the background of freezing my ass off (laughs) eighty feet in the air. Did it in my own way—I've always been kind of a maverick. I've come to meetings and had managers say, "Oh good, Joe's here. It's going to get done." You know, that's my drive, is to see a finished product. I don't know whether I'm weird or something, it's just me; I just love to see it happen. It's what gets me out of bed in the morning. Every day. Yeah. It makes me to go work. I just keep hammering away.

There's a big push to move things outside the company, which maybe looks good from an MBA standpoint, but as far as a produce-ability? It doesn't work. You're trying to take a company that's a world-class company putting out world-class products and saying, "Well, I don't think that's that technical of a job. Let's send it over to a nontechnical company." And so you've got this drawdown of the experience levels that you've built on for a hundred years, all at the stroke of a pen or a presentation. So hang on. We'll see how it goes in this country. We've basically offloaded most of our technical expertise out of the country, and it isn't just as easy as a point and a click. You have to be there to see it, put your hands on it, understand it, do it.

I used to really get a great feeling to see an airplane flying, or being delivered, or you know, knowing that because of what we do at this company we're connecting people throughout the world. Somebody wants to see their grandfather or somebody they haven't seen for a long time, and we've got an airplane that can transport them there safely. With this new airplane, don't have that feeling. Did you ever hear somebody say that? Just not feeling it. No, no, we're not building it. The Italians built the fuselage; the Japanese built the wings. And you can see it throughout the company, you know, the leadership has changed so many different ways—the upper leadership—went from being an airplane company, family-type orientation, three generations, to a corporation. And they let us know it by moving work outside. We had some really great leaders come through, and then they left. One guy was Alan Mulally. But Harry Stonecipher—yeah, real smart guy there, wanted to sell us out to GE. And what's really funny is, they think that the working-class folks don't understand these things. Well, once again, you get to that point where you start paying people too well, [and] they get really smart. Maybe they're too smart?

You know, I read articles about how in Japan the top CEOs make twenty times more than the lowest paid. In America it's four hundred times. That's where the Michael Moore guy comes in—that's his thing. He likes to come in there and jab them with his movies and his research, you know. Is it one-sided? Yeah. But was it needed? Very much so, because emotionally you believe in something, you'll do anything when corporations start becoming plastic, per se. They lose their humanity, human touch, you have revolt—that happens everywhere. So you know, I guess the only thing I can do in my little world of it all is to just keep toeing the line as a good citizen, good person, set the example. That's about all we can do. We hope that the leadership in the corporation would recognize it. They don't—not the current leadership. Very cold, calloused relationship now. That's probably what drove Mulally out, really, because he was a very personable person.

The minute Wall Street took over the corporation and basically put guys in and out like players on the chessboard, the dynamics are that we've changed the workforce. Instead of having the old-timers that are seasoned, they brought in new blood. They hire people off the street with no experience into this job that takes years and years of experience. Sometimes you look around the world and look at these corporations and look at the evil doings that go on, you know—this guy got a billion-dollar bonus, and he took away their health care; now they're suffering. We want a corporation like the Boeing Company or any corporation to be around to take care of us in our future years. You'd think that they'd have an obligation, a stake. I think that the future is going to get a lot harder. Corporations have an obligation: if they're going to set up shop in business, they need to step up and give back.

Everybody knows the quality of life is directly related to the quality of the product. A guy's making no money, he's going to not care what happens, not grow, you know. He makes his paycheck, he goes home, and he tries to survive. But when people—all the people in the whole group—are given enough opportunity in the quality of life you have quality of product. That's what's driven the company all these years, in my opinion. You know, the company doesn't realize just how important having people that want to do something, you know, be engaged employees. It's really sad. It's sad to see a corporation that could be putting out seventeen airplanes a day during wartime, to barely even making two a month.

The horror stories I hear from my friends that work outside . . . I mean just the latest, the crane that fell apart down here in Seattle, you know, killed a guy. If they're nonunion they're so worried about keeping the job or keeping the paycheck that they don't care. There's a good thing to say about unions, you know; they are organized, the workers are organized, and there is camaraderie amongst the union folks. If you're in a dangerous situation [outside a union], you know, nobody seems to really care. You die. People get hurt every day, and a union guy says, "Hey, we got to look out for each other; it's a brotherhood." The union guys know what they have. It's kind of like your family; you screw up in your family, the rest of the family gets on you. Don't screw up the family name. But they've taken that away from us pretty much now. And in the latest union-busting tactics, you know, it's a lie.

The relationships you have with people within the company is incredible, you know, and you meet up with people, just out of the blue, you'll work a project with somebody. The synergy's right there, and that's the cool part about it. That's what makes it what it is . . . just solving problems, just being the guy without the four-year degree that can look at something and go, "Gosh, why don't you try that?" And so I'm just standing there, you know, trying to figure this out. I'm looking up at the ceiling, just staring at the ceiling, and I look at the other guy, he goes, "Why don't you use a truss?" Bing. There it was. So it was like the coolest thing, you know. Now they use a laser. The cool thing is seeing the technology move ahead—being able to say, "I got involved in that." Some people enjoy actually building stuff and making stuff, yeah. Being grateful, that's a big issue. You've got to experience every single bit of your life, every moment you can, and enjoy it.

Part III

Newly Hired at Boeing

In this final section, we hear from people employed with Boeing fewer than five years. Unlike the retired or still working employees, these newly hired employees came to the company some ten years following the 1997 merger with McDonnell Douglas. They have never personally known Heritage Boeing; their leaders have not referred to the company as "family," and their organization has always been headquartered in Chicago rather than in Seattle. Even though not all newly hired workers are young, the young new hires are, in many respects, the future of the company. They are replacing, and will increasingly replace, the large cohort of long-serving baby boomers who are about to retire. This transition poses a challenge for Boeing. Can it manage the transition successfully so that decades of accumulated knowledge gained in designing and making airplanes are not lost but transferred across the generations? Hearing from new hires can help us answer this crucial question, as well as give us some indication of how successful the company has been in promoting its new vision, ethos, and culture.

We define new hires as those hired in 2007 or after—a period that coincides with a Boeing hiring binge and the "Great Recession." As thousands of workers were added to the Boeing workforce to support the development of the new 787 program and the ramp-up in 737 production, the national economy went into a tailspin. The national unemployment rate doubled from 5 percent at the end of 2007 to 10 percent in late 2009, with construction and manufacturing hardest hit and experiencing the largest employment drops since World War II. The employment of young men fell, job openings declined (from a peak of 4.8 million in March 2007 to a low of 2.1 million in July 2009), wage growth slowed, and the unemployment rate for engineers rose.[1] With such turmoil roiling the national economy, Boeing must have seemed like a welcome and attractive refuge for those entering the workforce for the first time and for casualties of the poor economic conditions.

How did these new hires embrace and/or adjust to Boeing's post-merger corporate identity and culture? How, in particular, did young workers connect with and respond to the new Boeing? Scholars, consultants, and casual writers have highlighted—and often lamented—the character and work dispositions that Gen Y employees (born between 1982 and 2000) bring to their jobs.[2] Painted with a broad brush, Gen Ys are said to have been pampered and sheltered by parents and schools who have cultivated an achievement-oriented, team-oriented, confident, trusting, optimistic, but often "entitled" generation. Gen Y is described as less loyal to organizations and more difficult to retain; they expect attention, mentoring, and good opportunities to develop their skill sets, which they then readily transfer to greener pastures when the mood strikes. Having seen the erosion of work benefits, longer work hours, corporations oriented more toward shareholders than toward stakeholders, and parents negatively impacted by downsizing, it is little wonder that this generation has decided they will neither spend as much time at work nor derive as much personal identity from what they do. Unlike members of previous generations, who might still hold out hope for a return to the good old days, Gen Y knows that the old social contract between workers and companies is a thing of the past. And yet, they also expect a meaningful career, one with balance, flexibility, and an understanding supervisor.

The interviews in this section do at times reveal aspects of this generational caricature. It is a subtle shift, one that likely reflects a youthful mind-set as well as any sociological transformation. Yet there are differences that reveal the emergence of a new way to think about one's employer and work life. Their comments on Boeing's business decisions and its emphasis on shareholder value suggest that they accept them as the "new normal." (And perhaps it is really no longer "new." This is simply what companies do, period.) Moreover, on the occasions when they are critical, their reactions and reasoning differ from those of veteran employees. Rarely does their tenor imply loss or nostalgia about a former way of doing business: those who dislike these corporate practices and values find ways of disconnecting from them, often with seemingly little emotional difficulty as compared to those employees we saw in previous chapters. Unlike members of previous generations who worry that the loss of innovation will compromise the company's long-term prosperity and competitiveness, these younger workers emphasize instead how they have been personally impacted in finding their work less fulfilling, meaningful, and creative.

We also find that Gen Y's sense of job meaning, involvement, and satisfaction frequently hinges on how well they have been mentored by their supervisors and supported by their coworkers. More so than with the older and longer-tenured employees, the happiness of the Gen Y individuals in this section seems to rise and fall with the quality of the support they receive and their ability to make a difference, even if it's only a small contribution to the work group. And yet, in the 2013 survey results, we find that newly hired Gen Y employees express greater levels of individualism: to the statement "I'd rather depend on myself than others," some 80 percent "agreed or strongly agreed," as compared to 71 percent (Gen Xers, born between 1965 and 1981) and 66 percent (baby boomers, born between 1946 and 1964) of newly hired older workers. This seeming paradox—the desire to be mentored and the desire to be independent—poses a tricky balance for organizations to achieve. Boeing seems to have dealt with it, in part, by making ample opportunities available while leaving it fully up to the employee to make use of such prospects.

Gen Y is also sometimes characterized as "working to live," not "living to work." Our survey data detected generational differences on measures of work effort that were consistent with this portrayal. For example, when asked, "What percentage of the day do you work to your full potential?" newly hired Gen Y workers answered 66 percent, as contrasted with 75 percent (Gen X) and 76 percent (baby boomers) of newly hired older workers. We found the same patterns for questions like "I usually show up for work a little early to get things ready" and "I only miss work when necessary." To this latter question, 71 percent of Gen Ys "agreed or strongly agreed" as compared to 80 percent and 86 percent for the newly hired older generations.

As we noted earlier, not all newly hired workers come from this Gen Y cohort,[3] leading us to ask, how do older newly hired workers regard the company? In what ways do they differ from their similarly aged contemporaries who worked for Boeing during the merger, and what does this tell us about the company's success in creating a new corporate identity and ethos? Unlike employees with long company tenure, who had to adapt and readjust their emotional ties to the company, these newly hired baby boomer or Gen X workers are "fresh" and unscarred by the events surrounding the loss of Boeing family or the move of corporate headquarters. Today's company is the only Boeing they've known firsthand. Is their basis for work and organizational connection different from that of Heritage Boeing employees? How do their previous work experiences shape the way they view Boeing's culture and corporate values?

Again, the 2013 survey data shed some light on these questions. Examining attitudes toward Boeing's culture—to what extent it creates a sense of purpose and meaning, fosters an atmosphere of trust and respect, or encourages innovation and creativity—newly hired Gen Xers and baby boomers almost always rate the company more positively than members of those generations who joined the company before or shortly after the merger. For example, to the statement "Boeing offers a compelling vision for the company's future," some 37 percent of newly hired baby boomers "agreed" or "strongly agreed," as contrasted with only 17 percent of those hired before 1996. We found similar differences for statements related to organizational support ("Boeing appreciates extra effort from me"; 30 versus 20 percent) and work effort ("Percent of day work to fullest potential"; 76 versus 70 percent). And as the interviews reveal, newly hired older workers express gratitude for their Boeing employment, the chance at a second career, and, more to the point, a well-paying job in a difficult economy.

In short, among newly hired workers, we see some generational differences, with younger employees reporting slightly less job involvement, engagement, and identification. Moreover, within the older generational cohorts, we find some lingering negative impacts of living through the turbulent time of the late 1990s and early 2000s. Against these differences, however, we find that overall, many of the attitudes among all recently hired employees are more positive than among those who lived through the merger and immediate postmerger changes. Although this is good news for the company and its employees, the news is not uniformly rosy. Employees report that they are satisfied with their jobs and do not plan to quit. But many of their feelings about the company—their commitment, how they see the company's culture, the degree of support they feel they receive from Boeing, and how engaged and involved they are with their work—are neutral at best or are strongly negative. As we see in the first chapter of this section, not all newly hired employees feel this way; however, the overall picture from the survey is far from ideal. We wonder to what extent these sentiments will, over time, erode the company's ability to retain its skilled workforce, especially if and when the economy more fully recovers and workers perceive greater opportunity elsewhere.

8

A BRIGHT FUTURE

Optimism about the future characterizes this group of young new hires. They feel confident they can build long careers at Boeing and are eagerly taking advantage of the "endless opportunities" the company provides. Whether it's doing degree work at a local college or taking classes through the "green light" system within Boeing, they are investing time and effort into developing their skills and education with the expectation that there will be a payoff in the future. One thinks it is "awesome" that Boeing pays for college classes and "amazing" that you can be hired by Boeing without much previous aerospace experience and still "make your dreams happen."

Like many others at Boeing, they told us that they appreciate the decent pay and the excellent benefits that are "still a pretty good deal," even with the end of defined pension benefits. On the whole, they find their work engaging (and if it isn't, they find ways to make it so by moving to other jobs within the company) and their coworkers helpful, supportive, and fun to be around. All are clearly proud of building safe airplanes that "your family could be flying on" and often voice pride in the company, reminiscent of employees who have a much longer tenure with Boeing. When they see problems or find faults, it is from the perspective of identifying obstacles to company efficiency and good communication.

Indeed, relative to other employees we interviewed, there is a noticeable absence of complaints or criticism of top management and the new business model. Rather, we see an acceptance that the company is just trying to "stay competitive with Airbus and all the new people coming into the airplane business." As one employee put it, "The company's number one goal is profits. I know it sounds cold, but it's true. I don't think there is anything wrong with that." Such pro-company attitudes, however, don't translate to antiunion sentiments for most of this group. Many value the role unions play in winning and safeguarding the good pay and benefits, with one actually changing his view of unions from indifference to appreciating the benefits of having a countervailing force to balance the power of management. These positive views of unions are tempered by a streak of independence that pushes them to resist any heavy-handed tactics to influence their votes in contract negotiations and by a desire for unions to avoid confrontation and to work with management to safeguard the company and future work.

SEAN ROOT

> There's something cool about being a Boeing worker.
> —Mechanic, age twenty-seven, one and a half years at Boeing,
> interviewed in 2014

My dad, who's worked at Boeing for over thirty years, had been begging me to come into the company for however long. Finally I gave in and sent out my resume to every position that they had on the website. The job application was designed to blanket everything. I had a preconception of Boeing workers, mostly from my dad. I just remember him complaining about all these workers who get nasty and mean with him, him being a manager. I've met quite a few employees outside from interacting with my dad, and they kind of feel like they're actually entitled to something and they offer little to the company. They're the ones that give that perception of Boeing workers. It was a turnoff. But now there are a lot of new workers.

My first impression of Boeing was that it was the best place I've ever worked. The attitudes were just amazing; it was a fun place to work. We tackled challenges together; we had each other's back. Just a fantastic place to work. Everybody respected the team leader; it was an earned kind of respect. He was very knowledgeable, and he'd go out of this way to teach you how to build an airplane. He took a lot of people under his wings, looked out for them, and generally cared about his coworkers.

I learn something new every week. It's not repetitive, more problem solving. When I was in fabrication, you're making the same parts every day; it was predictable. Where I'm at now, there's a lot more unpredictability; we got a lot of factory shop work going on, different challenges. I like that. It keeps me interested and engaged. I get more pride being a Boeing worker than being a machinist.

I plan to stay at Boeing. It would be foolish not to. You can't beat the wages or the benefits. I hope to be in either some sort of leadership role or something a lot more technical than what I am doing now. They have all sorts of joint programs and classes about airplane building. They call the classes "get your green lights on," because when you pull up this screen on career exploration on the joint programs site, what jobs you qualify for, it's green, so they call them "green light." I've been doing that pretty much every weekend, and I'm going back to school for a couple of certificates. Boeing's paying for it. It's awesome. I've met kids in the factory with no work experience. They got the job right after high school. It's amazing how they got the job; you think they'd need some work experience out in the real world . . . but no. You come into a company and can make your dreams happen.

I don't think Boeing's going to go away from Puget Sound anytime soon. If they do, it will be after my time with the company. I'm going to be here for a long time. You don't really have to worry about layoffs because if Boeing laid me off today, I'd still feel secure because now I have two job codes under my belt. With the union rules, I have the right to downgrade. I would probably just take a cut in pay and go work somewhere else. But I'd still be working.

The company's number one goal is profits. I know it sounds cold, but it's true. I don't think there is anything wrong with that. You know, if I was running a company, yeah, I gotta look out for my profit margins because that reflects the health of the company. Workers rank right below that. Without the workers we wouldn't be having these record-breaking share values. They [show how they value workers] with the best benefits in Puget Sound, the best wages, and they've got an incentive program handing out high points and all these things. A lot of these managers also tell you how much they appreciate your work.

I think everybody at Boeing feels like they make a quality product—I don't think there's too much of a worry with how well we make airplanes. I appreciate the attention to detail as I am afraid of flying, and so (laughs), as long as I know everything's been done well, it's always good to know everybody takes pride in their work, or most of them take pride in their work. The guys that don't take pride in their work are probably not working on something that critical or that important. Boeing looks for the good talent; they put them in the most important spots.

I just want to be known as the guy that could be counted on; the guy that has everybody's back, not just with the work but with interacting. I want to be trusted and respected. I'm pretty hopeful right now. There are a lot of jobs coming back to the United States. I feel positive about the job growth and the mentality of the people. I think we're going to see growth. There's something cool about being a Boeing worker. For me it's building airplanes. I'm excited to show up to work. There's some bad and nasty things at Boeing, but with all the cool things that we get to do, all the good things, it's fun to show up to work. It's pretty exciting to work there.

BERT WINSLY

> But I'm definitely proud of working for Boeing. I'm excited about the future. I'm excited to be with the company. I think the day I got hired, I got the phone call, was one of the happier days of my life.
> —Manufacturing engineer, approximate age twenty-five,
> thirteen months at Boeing, interviewed in 2012

I was hired in 2011, barely over a year ago now. I didn't have any professional aviation experience, but I'm an amateur pilot. I always knew this was where I wanted to come. I probably applied for over two hundred Boeing jobs before getting an interview. My older brother loves working for Boeing. He is a quality assurance specialist and actually also works in flight test. We don't often work together. I also grew up in Everett, so a lot of friends' parents worked for Boeing. It wasn't anything real foreign to me. I am a manufacturing engineer for a flight-test program. I went to eight weeks of manufacturing-engineering school at a Boeing facility to learn all of the computer programs and

Boeing-specific processes that we use. So I was two months into my Boeing employment before I ever really started working for Boeing. And I did like that transition and introduction to the company.

My actual job is a little different than I expected. I had gaudy expectations that I'm going to, you know, come right in and make a difference. I'm going to be doing high-level-type stuff. But most of what I do is a lot of paperwork, not the sort of engineering that you study at university. It's less challenging. Completely different skills are needed than what was needed for the degree in engineering. It seems obvious now, but I had to come to that realization. It took maybe six months after those classes to actually start earning some more responsibilities and to start making a difference. And that's sort of when it happened for me. When you're not only learning from people in your group but you can actually teach some lessons and actually start to feel you're a contributing member. I also got to do some traveling for the company and worked on the airplanes. That's when I really started to feel like a Boeing guy.

In flight test, we get a different amount of airplanes every week. Some weeks I'll work sixty hours, and then, two weeks later, I'm sitting on my hands trying to find something to do. I definitely wasn't expecting that. When it's busy, it's fast paced, it's "get it done," it's very stressful. When it is slow, it is "find something to do." I see a lot of differences among the employees. There are motivated persons who are hardworking and some who are just squeezing by, just hanging on, just fine having a job and are not necessarily fully committed. Before I came in, I heard about "the lazy B"—Boeing employees "do nothing"—and I have friends who work in this job who say on Facebook, "Doing nothing today." I know that happens, but that is not the dominant culture here. There are definitely more motivated, hardworking people than there are people hanging on and just happy to be here. That's a pleasant difference.

I would like a clear line, to go home and not think about work until I came back. I understand that that's not reality in any sort of profession. You do get the phone calls at home. You do have to come in on weekends sometimes, get stuff done. There are pluses and minuses. Obviously, if you're working more hours, you get more pay. But then there's increased stress and lack of family life. I'm not really too concerned about family life right now, being single. It doesn't have much of an effect on me if I work six weekends in a row. But it's not ideal.

My view on unions has changed pretty drastically. I might have been, I wouldn't say antiunion, but sort of didn't really care. I heard about strikes and thought, "Whatever, just go back to work," or "They want more money?" But now that I'm a part of it, and this probably is not unique to me, I can see the benefit a little more, having spoken with people who are longtime SPEEA employees, who can sort of see the push and pull between the company and the labor organizations. Labor organizations' goal, as far as I can tell, is to get us the best deal they possibly can. And the company's number one goal is to make the company the most profitable it can be, and that includes, "Spend less on wages." There are benefits to that kind of push and pull. I don't know what an unrepresented workforce would mean. I know that there are Boeing facilities in the United States that are nonunion, but I'm unfamiliar with what their wages are like. I don't know if I would jump ship and move to South Carolina and leave the union. I'd have to do a lot of investigating, a lot of research. I do have some worries, especially with this union and the contract negotiations. It's hard to save three or four months' worth of rent and bills. A strike wouldn't deter me. Even if we struck for two to three months every four or five years, I think that a well-disciplined person could survive something like that if it meant better wages. In the long term, it would definitely pay for itself.

If money wasn't a concern, I'd probably go back and be a pilot. Those jobs are extremely low paying. But I'm definitely proud of working for Boeing. I'm excited about the future. I'm excited to be with the company. I think the day I got hired, I got the phone call, was one of the happier days of my life.

TED SUCHER

> I hope my kids work for Boeing.
> —Machinist, age twenty-six, two years at Boeing,
> interviewed in 2013

My grandfather worked for Boeing for, like, fifty years. And my uncle worked at Boeing. This is a completely different career path for me.

Before this I was in construction, moving from job to job. I just wanted to try something new. So I wasn't really sure what to expect. I'm a steel tank sealer. I work on the wings; I go out and look at the actual planes being built. Basically climbing inside the wing and using steel to make sure the fuel tank doesn't leak. I was hoping to move around a little bit and, you know, move up a little bit and get a little more experience on how planes are built. I've seen opportunities, but I'm in a comfortable position right now, so I haven't looked at moving yet. But in the near future that will be an option. I expect a long-term career. There's definitely a lot of job security, so I'm happy with that. I'm happy with the health and pension benefits too. That was another reason for moving from where I was. I had no benefits or anything whatsoever, and my son was born about a couple months before I started at Boeing. That was a big reason to move, not only for my wife but for my son, just the family. I didn't get that in construction (laughs).

A hundred and forty thousand people at Boeing. You're just a Boeing drone (laughs). You kinda get what you expect, you know. And you're just a machinist. There are friendly people. Obviously work does get done. On the other hand you can still laugh and talk with other people and get to know them. We spend seven hours stuck next to each other a day (laughs). You learn a lot about somebody when you're around each other so much. We're a small shop; there are forty of us in our shop. You can even say we're a small family. We know a lot about each other. There are different work styles. Some prefer to finish their job a little bit earlier, and there's others take time, but you still get the same results. As a shop, we strive to meet goals, and when we do meet those goals, we get maybe a breakfast or a lunch or some sort of incentive. We've been told that we are the best steelers, probably in the world. We've had shops from Japan come to our shops just to see how we work so they can improve their work.

I'm right in the middle of the wing. I have one person on one side and one on the other; spending all day with each other and working next to those people is pretty much the ones I interact with the most. Others I see maybe during lunchtime or break time. "Hey! How's it going? How you doing?" (laughs). Yeah, we do have a lot of fun. We might play a joke, you know, use zip ties to strap things. Just a while ago there was people trying to tie each other's backpacks to the chairs (laughs). It kinda makes your day go by a little bit faster. Working by yourself, all day, you get bored, and you run out of things to think about (laughs). We all work together, and we just really stand united. For example, if we see that one guy is lagging behind a bit, we think if we finish a little early, I can go help him finish and get it done. Otherwise that bar doesn't get done; that's one wing we're not able to send down. We have to drop it down a day, and it gets behind, and it's just a chain reaction, you know, and work gets behind.

A lot of the people I work with, their mom worked there, their aunt worked there, their grandmother worked there. Boeing does value their employees' families. Last summer I was able to actually bring my family down and show them what I do. You see, when I come home, I can't describe what I do in words, but to show them, it's just really impressive. It's the family day. They have stuff open to have kids play on and handouts.

[If asked] I say I work at Boeing and build airplanes. Pretty proud actually. It's one of the biggest companies in Washington, and not many people I know actually work at Boeing. I was sitting outside with someone watching the planes take off, and we both had the same thought— "Oh yeah, that's something that we built"—and it's cool to see them take off. And it makes me feel good when we're driving around and my kids are like, "Hey Daddy! It's an airplane! Did you build that?" So I go, "I don't know" (laughs). I don't know—there's quite a few up there. So maybe I did, but, you know, it makes me feel good. If you don't do your job the right way and there are problems with the airplane later on . . . your family could be flying on this plane. So I always think about that.

The union is working with Boeing to try to provide the best pay, the best benefits, for us. You know, I don't know a lot about the union. I rarely see their Renton representative. There are union stewards by our shops. If I have a question, an issue, I can always go to them. But other than that . . . (laughs), that's it. I think unions are an important part of every job. They give you the best pay. They pay you what you want. I was never union before in construction, and I had minimal pay and no benefits. That's one of the things I was looking for going to Boeing, that it was union. They're there if I need them. The union is very, very strongly represented. I mean anywhere you go, stickers, shirts, all types of memorabilia. I even got told once by one of the old-timers a month after I started to stop working through my break because the union fought hard for it (laughs).

My goals? I don't know. Make enough money. Get bigger toys, bigger house. Support my family. And just to see what the future holds, how the technology of airplanes advances. I want to be remembered as a hard worker in all the careers I've been in. Just that I've been a good person, a good worker and take pride in my work. Boeing is a generational family. You are reminded of ancestors working for Boeing. I hope my kids work for Boeing.

CONRAD GAINES

> Boeing's overall goal is to make money, to stay open, and, you know, make sure they can stay competitive with Airbus and all the new people coming into the airplane business.
> —Mechanic, age thirty, two and a half years at Boeing, interviewed in 2014

I've lived in the area my whole life and heard that it is a great place to work, with great benefits and great career opportunities. A couple of friends that work at Boeing told me to apply. There were probably one thousand of us in the orientation class for new hires. The union representatives and managers told us what we were getting into, what to expect in the training, what to expect on the floor, where we were going, and just getting us ready for life after training. I was told during that you will be held accountable for everything, do not hide defects, and basically if you know something is wrong, tell somebody. But the accountability of your workmanship isn't enforced as much as I was led to believe. I'm very proud of my workmanship and work ethic, and sometimes it seems like some people go, "Oh, somebody else will deal with it." To me that's not right. The first days on the line were great. Everybody on my team was real helpful, trying to teach you exactly how day-to-day operations go. The team leads were amazing; anytime you have a problem, they are there to help. Yeah, it was great; everyone was really helpful right off the bat.

I'm at the very end of the line, before it goes out the door. We have flow days that the plane goes into each day. I'm on flow day eight; nine is the last one. We catch stuff that should have been caught earlier on in the line, and you're just like, "How did this make it this far?" But on the flip side, we caught this. I feel like it's my crew and my QAs [quality assurance] and the customer all working together who catch all of this stuff. It makes me feel a lot better about flying just because I know we have the best at the end of the line catching any defects.

It's an amazing place to work. I don't know of too many other places where you're building something millions of people are going to be on, and it's eye opening if you really stop and think about what we're really doing there; we're building the number one best-selling airplane that's out there. We want it to be safe, and I get the opportunity to work on it. So every day, I'm happy to go to work so I can help myself and all those other people that need to get from place to place on one of these planes. I'm sure not everybody feels that way. It just makes me proud every time a plane takes off at Renton Field. Saying, "Hey, we did a good job. This one is taking off. Let's get on the next one and try again."

I'd love to stay at Boeing. What I'd really like to do is start at the very beginning of the production line from day one and work all the way through and then even out to the field. That's my goal; to start at one end of the building and work all the way through. That way I get a better grasp of the whole production process. Then I can travel all over the world helping our customers with the problems that they have with our planes; go out there and make the things right that either we messed up or if they just need help on something. I'd like to make sure we have a satisfied customer.

There are endless opportunities at the company. I have never been so grateful to work for a company. Right now I'm trying to get my bachelor's degree, and the company and the union together are paying for me to actually go back to college on my own time; they are paying for everything. Most companies I've worked for are like, "If you want to go back to college, that's great, but it's out of your own pocket." Also the union and Boeing work together so well on giving you career opportunities inside of Boeing with what they call their "green light" system to tell you what classes you need to take within Boeing to forward your career.

It doesn't matter what my job is; I'm going to give all I have to that job while I'm there. I'm going to be there until the work is done and done right, so yes, it impacts my personal life outside work. I actually got my fiancée at work. The only time it's really negative is when we're really far behind because we can't get parts. Then it cuts into my family time. But to be honest, since we've been ramping up, I've been working less overtime, so it hasn't been that big of an impact. I'm really proud that I build the 737; that to me is the most important plane because we're putting a plane out a day on my line. To me that's impressive. People talk about how large all the other planes are, but when you're putting out a plane a day, it's pretty impressive to me.

I usually feel pretty good about the union. I've never personally dealt with it, but I know a couple of the people that I've worked with have had issues or have made comments about it. But besides that, it's a pretty good deal. There's good and bad in the [2014] contract. It's all a point of view, you know, because Boeing might have been bluffing; they might not have moved because of the whole 787 South Carolina stuff. But on the flip side, they could have very well just said, "Okay, well, we're moving the 777 elsewhere." So it's kinda a rock and hard place. Opinion was pretty divided; there were people that were for it and people who were against it. Even on my team there were people like that, but for the most part we came together and kept doing what we do every day: you know, build the planes and make sure they go out to the customers on time; keep the obligations we already have. I have no problem with whatever your opinion is, but you don't have to go around telling, "You better vote this way," or "You have to do this," or wasting your work time when you could be working. Have your own opinion, talk to people on your break time, but let's do our jobs. Do it on your own time, and if I tell you I'm going to vote how I'm going to vote, I don't really care what you have to say.

In my opinion, the company is just trying to do what's best for them, and we're getting really good wages for what we do. They pay us well. Yes, I wish we still had our pension and could continue growing our pension, but, you know, with the amount of time off we get a year and all the other benefits, it's still a pretty good deal. Boeing's overall goal is to make money, to stay open, and make sure they can stay competitive with Airbus and all the new people coming into the airplane business. They are just trying to run their company the best way for them. So I don't think there's a clear message from them saying, "We're going to break the union" or any of that stuff. I'm just thinking they are trying to get the best deal that's going to make the most money, keep the business open, keep us employed, and, you know, just keep Boeing going for hopefully another one hundred years.

I know we have some customers that are like, "We're all about the quality." Boeing has the quality, and I'm not sure what Airbus or Bombardier or any of the other new competitors have for warranties or guarantees, and I'm not sure how their inspection processes work. But I think a lot of customers do come to Boeing because of what our warranties are, and that they have the opportunity to come and watch the plane be built and inspect it while it's being built. And for the most part, just knowing that this company has been around for one hundred years and doing something right to keep it going that long. So I think that's definitely a big part of why the customers are with us. There's some that I'm sure we gave them a better deal on a larger number of orders, but for the most part I think it has to do with quality for sure.

I just hope that Boeing keeps hiring hard workers and that people don't start taking them for granted, because if we start taking them for granted, they can leave us at any time. People need to keep working hard, and I hope we can do it. I want people to think of me as someone who worked his hardest and put out the best product he was able to. I gave my all even when times were bleak and did my best to catch as many defects and put out the best product.

9

A SECOND CAREER

Starting a new career later in life can be difficult. One has to find ways to fit into a new workplace culture and to adapt to new ways of working and to new colleagues. But given the realities facing unemployed older workers, finding any job, especially one that has good benefits and decent pay, can seem like hitting the jackpot. That is certainly the case for the four individuals featured in this chapter. After being out of the labor force for between three and thirteen years (due to early retirement, taking care of an elderly relative, or losing a job because of offshoring or the recent recession), these individuals were immensely thankful to be given a second chance. They now had the opportunity to earn a living wage and rebuild their depleted savings. Linda Eames declares, "Abuse me all you want," to dramatize that she'd do almost anything to hold onto her new job, and George Sage notes, "After my experience, I'm happy to have any kind of job. I feel very fortunate."

One reason for such sentiments is the fact that unemployed workers who are over the age of fifty-five spend longer than any other group searching for work.[1] Moreover, an increasing number of employers have shifted to defined-contribution savings plans, such as 401(k)s, from defined benefit plans, thereby transferring the risk and volatility of retirement savings to employees.[2] Many individuals saw large drops in their retirement savings during the recent recession and associated drop in the stock market. This was the experience of Walt Austin, who "lost half of [his] money" in 2008. He and the others in this chapter are acutely conscious of the fragility of their situations and are determined to do all they can to hold on to their jobs and to increase their skills and employability.

The powerful sense of insecurity they feel, understandably based on their experiences, and their individualistic responses to their precarious situations, goes some way to explaining their jaundiced view of younger workers and the role of unions in the workplace. It is as if their experiences with life's uncertainty have taught them to play it safe: work hard, keep your head down, and don't ask for too much. Such attitudes certainly make them good employees from the perspective of the company.

WALT AUSTIN

> I went to Boeing because nobody else was rehiring, and quite frankly I needed a job. I need to get to sixty-seven: that's when I can get my Social Security. If the economy is really bad, I'll go until I'm seventy, which I won't particularly be looking forward to doing. But I'll do whatever I have to do.
> —Machinist, age sixty-two, one and a half years at Boeing, interviewed in 2014

I retired from my previous job after thirty years with a little bit of savings and a 401(k). They offered me almost a year of pay to take early retirement when I was almost fifty-five. I said, "Let me think about it," for about three seconds and then said yes. I was a network engineer at the time, so I was making on average a little over $70,000 a year. It was a good amount of money, so I left, and I thought I could make that last until Social Security, but the market crashed a year later, in 2008, and I lost half of my money. I used to install communication for the phone company before I became a network engineer. That's actually the best job I've ever had in my life. I thought I'd just go back to that, and I did that for about three and half months in the summer of 2008, but I got let go in October, and they never called me back. So I had to find another job, but it took me three years of going through unemployment.

I decided that I needed to do something else. I was looking to find something CAD, computer aided drafting, but it was way more expensive to go back to school than back in the seventies, when I got my degree, and I wasn't willing to part with $2,000 to $2,500 for three months' worth of education at that particular time. The economy was so bad at the end of 2010 they were giving out government grants to get people a fresh education. The unemployment office had me take a class; I took the machinist course and passed it in a year. Then I got a job. I went to Boeing because nobody else was rehiring, and quite frankly I needed a job. I need to get to sixty-seven: that's when I can get my Social Security. I've got five years to go; I'll be sixty-two in a couple of months, and I need to last. If the economy is really bad, I'll go until I'm seventy, which I won't particularly be looking forward to doing. But I'll do whatever I have to do.

The job is not particularly demanding. Everything is working with your hands—it's kind of similar to installing communication equipment, you know, building things, putting things together. The tools are different; the materials are different. Of course, I was on the '87 plane, which is a composite plane, so there's virtually no drilling to speak of; there's some. What I was trained for is enough drilling to last a lifetime. The things that come from South Carolina or out of San Antonio or Wichita, particularly South Carolina, either aren't put on the plane correctly or aren't on the plane at all, or there is an engineering change to remove them and replace them with something else. That's basically what I'm doing. It's just hands-on; it could be fixing a stump in your house. I've used hand tools my whole life. It's not physically demanding; it's not heavy lifting; it's not carrying a lot of heavy weight. It's like a very light version of manual labor. You have to be able to use a computer—just about everybody these days knows how to do that. You just have to learn the program, and I'm not having any issues with that, so it's neither hard work nor bad work. If you're busy, time goes by quickly, and you get paid for it. I'm not disappointed; I'm not thrilled to death, because I didn't really plan on working at this age. You know, it's like I said, "I gotta do what I gotta do." So I make that adjustment mentally. You know, if I was pissing and moaning, that's just not going to get you anywhere; you become a crappy employee and bitter, and I just don't want to deal with that. So I make up my mind that that's what I'm going to be, and that's what I do.

I knew that Boeing paid better than average. I knew that their benefits are better than average, but I was not aware that Boeing almost expects you to live there. I mean, there's overtime like you can't believe, and they'll make it mandatory if you're behind. They can make you work ten-hour days for up to three weeks, every single day, if they want to, if they need to, and then you get two days off, and then you start over. You do it again if you need to. I've worked mandatory overtime three times. Fortunately it was just five ten-hour days, and then I got a weekend, but overtime was available for those who wanted to work the weekend. Some of the younger folks took advantage of that, and they made an awful lot of money, even only making $15 or $16 an hour.

Boeing wants no unions. Basically, that's why they're in South Carolina. They start at $8, $9 an hour, where I'm starting at $15, $16 an hour. They want to pay as low as possible, and if the outsourcing thing had gone the way McNerney thought it was going to go, he probably would have got a bigger raise than he got. About three months before the battery fire incident, he got a 7 percent raise, and now that the 787 is for the most part starting to show some decent results, he got another raise. I don't know what the percentage was, but he makes over $21.5 million a year. Every year. So he can stand there on TV in his $500 Brooks Brothers overcoat on top of his $500 suit that he's wearing and talk about how the contract went smoothly and just the way they planned it. For the life of me, I don't know why they moved their headquarters out of Seattle. The place was founded in a building on Lake Union in Seattle; there's no reason for them to be in Chicago, none whatsoever. I think they got a tax break or something. And they continue to do stuff like that. I do know that McNerney will be retiring soon; he's sixty-five, and the word in the company is he's not going to be around more than a couple of years. Every time there's a changing of the guard, there could be a change of direction in the company as well. Who knows, maybe the new guy is a little more friendly towards the unions? If the push is to get rid of the union, then the unions need to try harder to get more members, which I'm sure they're aware of.

Young workers are a bit indifferent towards unions. If you were raised in a union household, which I was, you're more likely to be pro-union, although some employees that were raised that way don't like unions. They think unions are trying to screw them out of their money, but a union actually benefits the employees. Say you have a boss that's a bit of a bully, what are you gonna do? If you don't have a union, you're more likely to suffer or quit or get fired when you blow up and punch the guy. If you're in a union, you can tell him, "I'm going to get a steward," and that usually stops whatever is going on or at least resolves it.

I've worked for three young managers. One was twenty-four and one twenty-six. The third was twenty-three years old, and he sometimes acted like he was mature, and other times he acted like he was a sophomore in high school. It was difficult working for him; he only cared about the immediate task at hand. See, here's a thing that most people don't know: every single little thing that goes on in an airplane has a job number. Every little fastener, every screw, every washer, nut, bolt, everything has a job number. The place it's going to be on the plane has associated work tied to it that requires quality control to come. Each step requires someone from quality to come and look at it and verify that you did it correctly. I'm not used to working like that. At the phone company, when you install, you just do the work until you're done. There isn't anybody looking over your shoulder like there is at Boeing. Now granted, the phone company isn't going to kill 250 people if my little piece of equipment decides to blow up. So I can see the point of having that done, but having to work like that and then having your supervisor so focused on that part of the job was a little unnerving for me initially. You work thirty years in one particular way, and it's hard to just step out of that and say, "Okay, I can work like this." It's going to take some adjusting. And [the twenty-three-year-old supervisor] wasn't willing to wait for the adjustment in my case. So we didn't get along particularly well. Why do they give these jobs to these kids? Why do they take these jobs? Maybe because they want the money, but if you're already making top pay, why would you put yourself through that aggravation? I've been in management; I've seen what that does to people. I don't want to do it again. They don't know; twenty-two-, twenty-three-year-old kid, he doesn't know. He thinks he does, but he doesn't. He'll realize when he's in his thirties how stupid he was when he was twenty-two because that's the way life is.

At work, many people will look at something someone did not quite right and say, "We gotta fix it," and we'll all look at each other and say, "How the hell do these things fly?" Something that weighs 180 tons doesn't belong in the air. It's kind of a joke. We laugh about it, but we fix it and make it right. And it's all good; it wouldn't get up in the air if it wasn't good. It's inspected by the quality people at Boeing; it's inspected by the FAA folks; they routinely come through the building.

Sometimes they surprise you, sometimes they notify you in advance, but nothing gets up in the air unless it's able to get up in the air.

Right now I have a goal. I'm trying to find a way to get that CAD education and learn Boeing's software system called "Catia." I just found a job that's called technical design, that's actually a SPEEA-engineering-union-type job that pays $92,000 a year, but I'm a little leery because they're moving a lot of them to California at the moment, so it might not be something I can do with Boeing. But if they're going to pay for the education, I'll get the education and not worry about layoffs, or if I choose to leave Boeing, then I can use it to get some other job locally. That's good enough for me. I'll take that opportunity. Going from $16 an hour to $92,000 a year is a pretty good objective, I would say. We'll see what happens.

LINDA EAMES

> I didn't work for six years before I got the job at Boeing because I had to take care of my mother. I looked at her financial situation, and when Boeing offered me the job, I was not about to turn it down, because I knew, even at my advanced age, I could have money coming in in the form of a pension and better savings than I would get with an individualized 401(k).
>
> —Inspector, age fifty-two, one and a half years at Boeing,
> interviewed in 2014

When I started I was absolutely in a tailspin, overwhelmed by the size of the place—it was like a whole retraining on how to get to work on time—and just overwhelmed with everything. The first week I was just blown away. Getting up at 3:30 in the morning in order to get to the parking lot early to have a spot in the same zip code as where you work. It was rough trying to find a room number in the building, realizing that it's a tiny city. Lots of Boeing quirks. What's allowed, what's not allowed? I was surprised about safety glasses throughout the plant, no matter what. Normally you need them when you actually get to where you're working, but then again, with that many people, I understood why it happened. Also, Boeing has its own language. Everyone has to learn Boeing-ese. Big place, slow-moving wheels.

At this point, the only thing I won't do is dumpster-dive. I mean (laughs), I had to do that once in the army, and I hated it. So I'm not doing it again. But if my boss says, "Hey, I need you this weekend," I'm not gonna flinch. I don't work late on weeknights because I live alone and have a dog, and she's locked in the house for eleven hours every day. I need to be home on time to let her out, but on the weekends, abuse me all you want. If he says, "I need you to go to Structures," well, you know what? I go because I'm not stupid; I could learn there and become more valuable. My value becomes worthless once Boeing decides to write off x amount of people. But I fight the mind-set of "This is all I do." Oh no. I'm not gonna be that way.

I've had three layoff notices already, and when I started looking at the layoff lists, there were people with layoff notices that have been there since 1988. That said to me, "Well, OK, you are never secure in this job." I'm only two tests short of going two grades higher, and the company makes it very easy to do so. I found that to be absolutely delightful. But right now I'm not touching it because if I move up a grade, I'd be way at the bottom of their seniority list. So I'm staying right where I am until all this blows over. My whole goal in life is to keep moving toward the front door and then out the front door onto the frontlines, and I'd kind of like to be the person who hands someone the keys to their new plane, you know? I'd like to stay five years. I have to wait for my puppy to pass. I know I sound terrible, but I have to wait for her to pass before I can go to college and get my license.

Boeing's a very disheartening place to work some days. Like the guy who always wears dark suits and has his head down, never has anything good to say—"Daddy the Downer." That's the personality. Yeah, moves slow, shuffles his feet. The whole feeling that you get at Boeing, at least in my area is, it's pointless. That it doesn't matter to the company until something goes wrong. Then they are on you like a fly on poo. And it's your fault, and they call the FAA: "Get the FAA on this person because it's their fault." Part of that stems from their procedures and policies. You have layer upon layer upon layer of ways to do things. All those policies, all those procedures need to be combined into one stinkin' area. It's absolutely mind-boggling.

That's another big beef everyone has: "Oh, Boeing doesn't care if you get hurt!" Yeah they do, especially if you're doing something they expressly asked you not to. Right now there's a big thing going, and this is somewhat hearsay, but evidently a guy stepped on a relation pin, which is like a good two and a half to three inches long. Well, he didn't say anything to anyone for two days, and now he's losing his foot. Now he's agitated and going to Boeing and saying, "Hey, you guys owe me this money," and they're saying, "No, we don't. You didn't follow the rules. You did not tell anybody." Boeing's dead to rights on that one. They give all these opportunities, and people don't take them, and then they get PO'ed, and then I'm like, "It's your own damn fault." They try to give you things to make your job safer, and sometimes those things work, and sometimes they don't. Right now we're fighting having to wear bump caps all the time for a couple of reasons: one, you hit your head on something once on the job, your chance of doing it again are pretty slim. Two, it's adding an inch and a half of height. So now, where we could have stood up straight, we can't, and we may end up with some pretty serious neck injuries. It's just like, that's what they get in their head, and that's just how it has to be.

I'm putting more heart into work at Boeing than I did in construction. I'm very career focused, and work is highly important to me. But I'm not going to give my entire life to Boeing. I'm not going to work six days a week all the time. No, I exist, and in order for me to maintain a good career focus, in order to be a good employee who is not sick all the time, I need time off. So I'm going to take it. I think actually that my happiness levels have dipped a bit. I mean, I loved my job in construction. I absolutely loved it. In the construction industry, you're not confined to an aircraft hangar, whereas at Boeing, it's indoors, and everything is right there. That's the biggest thing for me: I'm not outside; I'm not seeing new people every day; I'm not driving around in the middle of the day. But I'll stay at Boeing, and this is the one point I'll give the union, because there's a good pension, and there's a good savings plan. I'm old, you know. I didn't work for six years before I got the job at Boeing because I had to take care of my mother. I looked at her financial situation, and when Boeing offered me the job, I was not about to turn it down, because I knew, even at my advanced age, I could have money coming in in the form of a pension and better savings than I would get with an individualized 401(k).

It's a male-oriented job, as was construction. I remember when my foot hits the factory floor that I am a woman first and foremost, and that does not make me stupid and that does not make me weak. I always try to remember who I am as an entire person. I thought Boeing would be a little more progressive, but they're evidently not. I enjoy interacting with the mechanics, being able to be yourself, because they're people too. They're not just stupid idiots sitting behind a wrench, you know; they're not. I'm pleasant even when they screw up. I see about 90 percent male, so you do a bit of flirting. Makes the day go by faster, and everybody is happy with it. They go home to their wives, and somebody says you're flirting with them, and they're happy. At my age, I'm not dead yet.

I'm finding that there are very clique-y groups. I just can't seem to fit into any of them. Well, there's the group that we have right now, where it's three or four inspectors, and they are the be-all and end-all, because they never have time to go on jobs, but they sure have time to just sit around and peruse the scene and find mistakes in everything everybody does. So it's like, "Remind me not to hang around with you." One of those guys is our union steward; he never works. "Why are you even here? I never see you on the board. You don't even tell me that you spend six hours a day doing union bull crap, 'cause if that's the case, the union steward needs to be someone hired by the union and only does union work. You are also an inspector. Get up off your fat ass and do something." Fuck. Sorry for the F-word. I was in the military when I was very young and very impressionable, and as a result my thing is, "You're at work. You're here to do a job. Get up off your butt and do it. Quit sitting around on YouTube. Quit sitting around playing on your cell phone. Do your damn job." That's my biggest personal beef. We have this girl, this female inspector. It's her first full-time job ever—she's like nineteen years old—and all she did was sit around and yap on her cell phone all day. You know, really?

This is the first union shop I've ever worked for in my life, which I know sounds weird, coming from Detroit. In my humble opinion I am absolutely disgusted by unions in that a lot of the people who need to go away, the ones that are constantly making mistakes, big mistakes that they've been counseled on before, they remain. I find it very distressing that Boeing will just throw out a number, get rid of all these people that are good, rather than weeding through the company and getting rid of the ones who deserve to go away. It's embarrassing to me to see people sit around all day with their finger in their nose and they make $32, $35 bucks an hour. I just think, "Why?" The union was a good idea back in the twenties when we had child labor and people working seven days a week. It was a good idea then, but unions are pretty much a thing of the past in a lot of different respects. Either that or the unions need to reorganize themselves and realize that they're not there to widen their own pockets. They act like our friend; they act like they're the best thing that's ever happened to you in the world, but you know, I worked for a lot of nonunion places, and I've had just as good benefits as I get at Boeing. A good portion of the people I've spoken to—let's say, if I took ten people, at least nine of them would say, "We don't need a union here." The union does nothing but get in our way. The union impedes progress. It doesn't allow for growth. How do I phrase it? In other places I've worked, if your boss said, "Go do this," you did it. You didn't go, "Oh, wait a minute. Let me see if it's in my contract." The mentality is "Screw it. I don't care. I'm getting paid. I'm union ha ha ha . . . I don't have to work to get my money. I'm union—they can't get rid of me." The sad part is there is a lot of truth in that statement.

I love Boeing for giving me the chance to be an aerospace inspector. I take my job very seriously. Plenty of nights I have lost sleep over my job because I've been concerned about something I did or possibly missed. Boeing and anyone who gets on an airplane will be happy I took the time I did to find flaws. Boeing's a good company, but I think that a lot of people from outside could come in and look at what they're doing and come up with something a little better as far as policies, procedures, and how to run the entire show. That's the one thing I would say to Boeing: "Dig it out of your butt. Think about what you're doing, and think about how you're going about it. Take the word from the employees, for Pete's sake, because if you're starting to get an overwhelming response, then maybe it's time to look at what you're doing and change it." Yeah, I guess people might say, "I'm a crabby ole bitch."

GEORGE SAGE

The first promotion you get is more than 10K, so that will be nice. But I'm not holding my breath. After my experience, I'm happy to have any kind of job, and I feel very fortunate.

—Technical designer, age sixty-five, one year at Boeing,
interviewed in 2013

I've been at Boeing for one year in the commercial side as a technical designer. It was very unusual to be hired at all at my age. During the recession, I know a lot of people who just had to retire because they lost their employment and couldn't find anything else. Before Boeing, I was a building contractor pretty much my whole life. I left my previous job because of the housing crash. I wasn't making any money anymore. I went and got a drafting degree. When I started going to school, most of the people there seemed to want to work for Boeing. They're the only large employer who hires drafters. My daughter told me about the company—they spent a lot of time training her. She had good experiences with the management. They seem to care about their employees. It took me a year to get hired, and I'm really happy with how I'm treated there.

I'm totally new. I spend half my time in training and have lots to learn. The software programs are difficult to learn, and there are so many of them. You're learning for years. My daughter has been there for a few years, and she is still not comfortable. Boeing values the development of their employees. There's been a lot of layoffs around me, but it's all been contractors. In general, because they spend so much training you, they really don't like to lay people off. There are unproductive people, but they don't get fired generally. The first promotion you get is more than 10K, so that will be nice, but I'm not holding my breath. After my experience, I'm happy to have any kind of job, and I feel very fortunate. I'm happy with where I am. I think I will stay at Boeing until I retire. In about five years, I'll reevaluate. It took me years to build up my clients, and they went bankrupt. I'm too old to start over again in the construction business.

I'm in engineering, so it's a lot of smart people. You have to be intelligent to do this, and sometimes I don't feel that smart. They encourage you to contribute, but you don't have much to contribute at first. I'm seen as the old white guy. They expect me to be experienced, but I'm still new. So I get some respect because of my age, but I don't know much about the business. They talk a lot about open culture here. There's always a gap between what's said and implementation, but I haven't seen any hypocrisy. If they say we want an open culture, they really try to implement that. I know people are more skeptical about these things. You have a lot of opportunity to listen to executives and speak to them, so that's been a source of information for me. I try to do that, but not everyone does. I've heard some things about how managers have a hard time managing young people. But I haven't seen any evidence of that. I see them as just as ambitious and eager as anyone.

I work in an open-cubicle office. And, you know, there are a lot of groups that don't really connect that much with each other. If we have to, we can talk to another group, but the lead does a lot of that. I'm mostly involved with the people in my group. We have team-building things once a quarter. We have office assistants, and they try to do things for us. You spend a lot of time staring at your computer. I just have one guy from my last team that I see socially. In this team, I don't see people socially. I have invited my lead to dinner once or twice, but we haven't yet. That may have been inappropriate in corporate culture.

I spend forty hours here, so it's a big part of my life, but I don't get much identity from it because it's a second career. I spent most of my life with my contracting business. Everything was built around that business. I was always very concerned with producing high-quality products. My clients were all high-end builders. It's the same here—I like their high quality. As a former carpenter, I'm concerned with craftsmanship. I've worked my whole life, so I'm very reliable. I've gotten great training from life coaches.

I'm not a big union guy; I'm pretty skeptical of unions but appreciative at the same time. I see how it can be helpful to have a union. It's odd for me to be in a union because I was the employer in the past. I often feel like what the company gives us is more than fair, and yet these hard-core union people didn't want to sign a contract, and they wanted to strike. I thought it was nuts. I don't understand unions very much. I don't have much experience with them. It seems like there's a lot of companies that seem to get by without unions. So I don't know.

I do identify with Boeing. I'm a loyal person, so I support the company. I just think of myself as someone who is in training and wondering when I'll be done with it. I feel like a student again. I love the quality of Boeing's products and the safety. There's a lot of pride here with what we do. I think that air travel is a contributor to a lot of the peace of the world and certainly contributes economically. Boeing is the number one exporter in the US. And I love travel, so it brings me joy to work here.

AMBER MASLIN

> With the way the economy is, you cannot foresee retiring at sixty-two
> or even at sixty-seven. [. . .] I used to think, "Yeah, I want to retire by
> the time I'm fifty," but when I got laid off and I couldn't find a
> permanent job, I ended up using all of my savings. So I have to put
> everything back.
> —Mechanic, age fifty-nine, one year, nine months at Boeing,
> interviewed in 2014

I got laid off in 2000. My job of twenty-two years went overseas, and
you just can't find a job anymore. I couldn't get a job anywhere for
many years. It was hard. I didn't even think I would get hired at Boeing,
knowing my age. I was doubtful, but I noticed that they do hire a lot of
older people mixed in with the younger generation. One day I just went
into the Tech Center; they had a fifty-plus courier fair, and I went
around it thinking, "Maybe I'll go back to school." I saw a composite
technician and decided to take a chance and try it. Went to Tech for six
months to get my certification and got hired at Boeing. I thought aerospace was the only way to go, you know, because I knew that Boeing
was hiring, but I didn't have that much experience. I do have a lot of
high-tech background, but not in aerospace. I didn't know what I was
going to get into. When I came into Boeing, I thought I was going to be
a composite technician, but it turns out they put you where they need
you. But it doesn't matter. It's great. I'd heard about Boeing before I
applied. I'd heard it had a great benefits and lots of good incentives. So
for me it is a great company.

I can see now, with the way things run, that Boeing treats its employees pretty well. They constantly give us incentives and take us out. I
didn't expect much of that because I thought, "Oh, you know, things are
coming down, the way the economy is." I was surprised. They encourage us to stay safe, and they reward people for being safety conscious.
The future for any company now is that they don't want to keep you,
but you're better off having a long-term employment at Boeing than
any other company out there. I see myself staying as long as I keep up
and learn more. They give you incentives to get certified, and then if I
see an opportunity, I can move to one. Because there are quite a lot of
jobs open across every field, it makes you think, "Oh, I can do this, or

you can be this." If you train and do well, then you're fine. I can just about go anywhere once I develop more learning.

I'm pretty much in the 787: we're building the wing part. I like it. I didn't think I would in the beginning. I had never worked that hard physical work. The tools were not that light; they were very powerful tools, automatic tools. It was hard because not very many women are in it; the majority of them are men. The guys have been there for twenty-five to thirty-five years, and they expect you to move just like them and that you'll pick it up really fast. But it wasn't that easy for me. They would say, "Do it," and I had a problem with that. They don't communicate as much to women or train the way that I thought I should be trained. You have to be strong, not only physically but strong-minded too, to be working with men. Men are rough-and-tumble. You know, you can tell some men think that women shouldn't be working in this area because they think we physically cannot handle it. But I think once you know the equipment and get used to it, then you'll be fine. You just need to find the right trainers. One guy was open. He gave me a tool he was using to turn a huge knob. He says, "Okay, now you can do it. I'll let you do it. I don't care what the other guys think." I did it, and he said, "Wow," because it was physically hard. He was willing to take a chance to make me try it. Eventually I got it. Now it's like a piece of cake.

Actually, for every fifteen to twenty men there is only one woman. I wish there were more women. Women can do it; it's just a matter of, can you handle the physical part? I think the younger ones coming in are more accepting. The older ones have a harder time. Some are very stubborn with old men attitudes. You just have to learn to fight back in a modest way, and they pretty much accept it back. But I know there are some things that women specifically cannot do. What I was told is that you always need people. So no matter how strong the other person is, you still need two people, to prevent injuries or accidents. Strong or not, you help each other.

I've actually been working ten-hour days, every week and every weekend. They make it mandatory now that you work two weekends in a row and one weekend off, so I'm very committed to that. I tell all my friends, "I can't go here." I've been missing family functions. I said, "I have to go to work," and with the way the situation is, I'd rather be working. With what I went through, you don't know the future. Work comes first. I really have to think that way. I don't like it, but you have to do it. As a matter of fact, I heard Boeing say that work comes first before family. That's what I heard . . . that's what is being said, and I said, "Really?" I was kind of taken by surprise. So you have to change your priorities. [. . .] Now I'm lucky because I'm single. I don't have any commitment to anyone.

I guess I have to accept being in a union, but at Boeing you have a choice: you don't have to be a union member, but you still have to pay dues. It's good and bad. I think the union is good for now. The thing about the union is they keep certain things straight labor-wise, but I think there are some parts where they can be greedy, and that can be hard because you know they get paid a lot. We pay, what, $70 a month in union dues, so they're making their millions. I don't know, I ask myself, "Do they even care about the rest of us?" I don't think so. When you look at the auto unions, they're doing exactly what the auto unions have done where eventually they phase the union out. I feel like it's gonna break the union. I think the evidence of that is that there are union members not trusting the leadership of the union. That's when you don't know what the future is. They might say, "We cannot pay this much. We'll go to another country." It's scary.

I'm at that age where I don't want to retire; I'm beginning to really like this. I'd rather be working than doing something else. So, yeah, I see myself working more. I don't mind staying another five, another ten years. As long as I'm physically healthy, I can do it. With the way the economy is, you cannot foresee retiring at sixty-two or even at sixty-seven. I don't know—it's so hard to tell. I used to think, "Yeah, I want to retire by the time I'm fifty," but when I got laid off and I couldn't find a permanent job, I ended up using all of my savings. So I have to put everything back. If I end up retiring now, "Oh my god, do I want to do all of this again?" Now that I like the job, I'm like, "Hey, I can go further than this. I don't have to stop and rely just on Social Security." I just wish I were younger (laughs).

I like to make a difference. I know one of these days I'm going to be riding on this plane. I want to make sure that that plane is done right. Making sure that I did a good job—build it better, doing it faster, but better quality is what I strive for. I'm very proud that I can do it. Because I thought, "Ah, God, this is hard physical work. How am I going to last a year? I don't know if I can do it." Now I can see myself working here more than five years. You constantly have to change and catch up. I'd like to be in more technical areas, electronic technician, or procurement; lighter work and lesser responsibility in procurement as an international buyer. It's been great for me, and you know, I always get excited to go to work; I always try to go in as early as possible. I just want to get there.

10

NOT WHAT I EXPECTED

"**E**xcited" and "motivated" are the words used by the employees interviewed in this chapter to describe how they felt when first hired by Boeing. They expected work that would be innovative and groundbreaking; they assumed they would "work hard"; they thought they'd be part of a team that worked together to build "cool" products. They felt "pretty damn lucky" to have landed such a good job at a large and important company and anticipated fulfilling employment.

Unhappily, however, all of these employees encountered work that has been uninteresting, inefficient, and slow. They have experienced contentious relationships and very little coworker camaraderie. They report being poorly mentored and/or receiving little career-development help. Moreover, they contend that their experience is symptomatic of the broader organizational culture, describing it as a "bland corporate environment" characterized by an old-fashioned, tedious, and bureaucratic way of working. It is also a "territorial" culture that doesn't value working together harmoniously. Besides pointing to their own experiences with their jobs and the workplace culture, these employees are highly critical of the company's business strategy, noting how, for example, the value Boeing places on investor earnings led to untold problems with the 787 or how increased production rate expectations have led to employee stress over meeting such untenable performance goals and, subsequently, poor workmanship.

In short, the employees in this chapter have failed to make a connection to the work itself, their coworkers, the company, or the profession.

In response, one worker has already left and returned to his old job, concluding that a company with these qualities is not "a good long-term investment." Another is looking to leave, and the remaining two employees are waiting to see if their fortunes somehow improve.

EMILY TAYLOR

> You don't trust the person to your left. You don't trust the person to your right. You don't say anything to anybody. I am not looking for another job per se, but I don't see Boeing as a long-term thing.
> —Mechanic in her early twenties, two years at Boeing,
> interviewed in 2013

I am a mechanic. I was initially hired in 2011 and have been at Boeing for almost two years. I had friends and family that worked there for years. My family always talked about liking their job; everybody enjoyed their job in my family, so I never thought twice about it. I trusted my family. I knew that Boeing offered good benefits. That it's a good place to work. A job is good to have in a bad economy. I expected that Boeing employees would be assertive and optimistic and work together to build a plane. It takes teamwork to build a plane, so I figured that Boeing must have good teamwork. When I was told that I was hired, that was probably one of the most exciting events of my life.

When I was in training, I thought it was super exciting. I was excited every day to go to work. I got done with training in four months, and then about a month after being out on the shop floor, I started to despise my job. When I was introduced to my shop, the manager who I was with would do anything for you as long as you did your job. He treated you really well, and it seemed like everybody worked together. Then after maybe two weeks, I started to get to know people around me and noticed their work ethic; there was no motivation. Nobody cared, and the manager I had—everybody really, really liked him—transferred to a different location, and we got a different manager, and ever since then, it has just been one bad manager after another.

Everybody feels that the only way that they are safe in their job is to show management that they are not union friendly. A lot of the managers come on really strong and aggressive, and it is a very threatening environment. Nobody works together. I mean, I could simply be doing one thing wrong, I can say one thing, and it's brought up as, like, discriminatory or offensive. Everybody feels like they need to tell on each other, to distract attention away from them, because the managers have made them believe that they will not have a job at the Boeing Company unless you show favor towards management.

It is miserable. I talked to a woman, and we saw her working really hard, and one person came up to her and is like, "You must be new." She is like, "I have been here about four months—how did you notice?" And they are, "Because you are working really hard, like, you are just constantly working." She never interacted with anybody; she was just constantly just doing her job, didn't screw off, just working, and then she told us that she had previously worked for a contractor for Boeing and she just knew her stuff and she really enjoyed doing her job. If I look at her now, she is a completely different person. She is just like the rest. She blends in with everybody else and nothing special, not that ace mechanic anymore. So you slowly watch the Boeing world take you over and put you into a really ugly person.

People tell me you used to get rewarded for stuff and told how much you were appreciated back in those times. It is not necessary, but I am pretty sure that I recall in psychology that you don't approach with negativity; you always approach with a positive aspect and follow with the negative. Say, "I really like the way you did this—that is awesome—but here's what you can work on." Thank you very much because I just worked really hard for you, and now you don't even appreciate it.

I feel like they have a really bad label on unions: that we are lazy, don't do anything because we have a freaking union to protect us, all that stuff. But I think it is a really good thing to have because it protects the people, and honestly, the people don't work any harder in nonunion jobs than they do in union jobs. From what I have seen in Charleston, honestly, they do the same exact things as the union members do. There is really no difference; it is just false allegations. You have a chance to fight for yourself. In Boeing Charleston, if I am portrayed as a crappy worker, they can just say they don't like me. "Hey, you didn't get your job done on time—we are walking you out. You are fired." Whereas if I am at Boeing, I have protection against someone like that.

McNerney has no experience in the aviation industry. It was a kind of thing where he basically went over a budget and decided, "Hey, we are going to spend less money on this airplane. We are going to outsource the crap out of these airplanes. We are going to get everything from Italy and dah dah dah." They want to make the company something new, something that you have never seen before. And it is not happening the way they thought it was, so their success rate with these new airplanes that are coming out are failing miserably, and it is becoming a really crappy environment. Obviously I am sure the CEO is not very happy with the rate of success that is happening, and he comes down on the VPs, who come down on the directors, who come down on their management, which pretty much pisses everybody off.

It seems like they are ramping up the rate in other programs, like they want planes delivered faster, and I hear employees complain, "How am I going to complete these jobs when you have nine hundred things you have to do extra all in that time span?" It stresses the crap out of the employees when you are afraid of doing something wrong, like when you are a little kid and your parents discipline you. Everybody is on edge at the company. They don't want to put in any effort for their manager because they do not care about their manager. It just wasn't expressed through training how critical these airplanes are. Because it is insane to know that a lot of people do some of the things that put millions of lives at risk because they are thinking about their manager reprimanding them for not getting this work done on time. So, basically you just got people busting things out quick because they are so afraid of being terminated for not getting it done on time.

I think it is the way it is today because most people aren't doing jobs that they love. Instead they are doing jobs to survive. If you asked me five years ago if I ever thought about working at the Boeing Company, I would probably tell you, "Hell no," because it wasn't my passion. Everybody is just looking for money right now. Happiness right now to people is money: it is not doing the job I love. I work at the Boeing Company so that I am not homeless. I had the option of staying in the military. I always say the Boeing Company is just like the army, but the only thing that they can't make you do is get down and do pushups.

My job is important to me because it puts food on the table; it allows me to have luxuries and go on vacation, do the things I enjoy, but I used to work a lot of overtime because I liked my manager. I liked my job when I liked my manager. Now I just say I work to live. I don't live to work. I don't put in the extra effort that I need to because if you treat me like crap, why should I help you succeed? If I was getting paid $10 an hour to do this job, maybe even $12, maybe I would quit this job or go look for another job. On to the next. When you are working at Pizza Hut when you are seventeen and your manager treats you like crap— you are like, "FU, man, I am out." If you are paying me just a little bit over what a freaking person makes to fold clothes, and I can have a better manager doing that, bye.

Benefits and pay is really the only thing the Boeing Company has to offer. I remember back in the day when my mom was an hourly employee: every day after work her whole crew would go out to the bar and hang out. If I even ask people to freaking do that these days, they would be like, "No, I got other things to do than freaking hang out with you." Nobody wants to hang out with each other. Everybody hates each other. Everybody just fakes a smile so that we can just get through the day. Nobody is friends. You don't trust the person to your left. You don't trust the person to your right. You don't say anything to anybody. I am not looking for another job per se, but I don't see Boeing as a long-term thing.

JARED CREW

> The problems are pretty fundamental to Boeing—so I'm trying to break my golden handcuffs and [am] looking outside the company for a new career! I think a lot of the problems are more or less symptoms of a gigantic, publicly traded manufacturing company.
> —Stress analyst, age twenty-three, one year at Boeing, interviewed in 2013

I did a three-month summer internship in 2011, and then I started again last year as a stress analyst. Both my internship and my full-time job have been with the same group—787 wing structures. When I joined the company, I was excited. It's a big brand, and it's cool. But during my internship, I was really bored for a lot of it because three months at an aerospace company is not enough time to actually accomplish anything realistic. They have a tough time with interns in terms of giving them meaningful assignments that keep them engaged and involved. I did a lot of menial work, which kind of sucked. But, well, I'm an intern, you know, whatever. It's fine, and so coming in as a full-time,

I was expecting to help work on designing the airplanes and doing the stress analysis.

I think the 787 partner system has created a very take-centric environment, where the partners are constantly negotiating with Boeing about resource allocation and work and all kinds of things like that. The negotiations are relatively formal, and the terms are explicitly defined. I think this has created habits that spread to the way engineering work is allocated within Boeing as well, making everybody protective over their own resources and relatively unwilling to do favors for others.

There is a lot of stuff that doesn't totally make sense, and my work doesn't give me energy or pleasure. Most of what I do is very disconnected from the final product, and I'm doing it because some piece of paper says it's necessary. Aerospace is full of rules, and Boeing just adds to them. There are a lot of liability-limiting rules, like how we're not allowed to put anything on top of our file cabinets, because in an earthquake they could fall and hit somebody or fall and impede evacuation routes. This includes pieces of paper. Or there are no food trucks allowed to serve Boeing in Everett because they pose a terrorist risk or something. It's ridiculous.

At school I took some classes on leadership, which were super interesting, and based on that knowledge I've noticed there are very few good leaders here. Within management I don't know of any good leaders who are first or second line. My third-line manager is a good leader though. And some engineering leads are decent leaders, but that's relatively infrequent too. I think one of the reasons Boeing has poor quality in its managers, other than poor incentives, is that it takes around ten-plus years to become a manager. While at some companies that could be used to vet out all the poor candidates, at Boeing it means all the good candidates leave, and you're just left with whoever wants to take the position.

Staffing decisions are done based on spreadsheets; engineers are treated as a pure commodity. Within a group, assignments are given to specific people based on expertise, but for entry-level engineers, the assumption is that we come in knowing nothing, and we only learn things through experience. But the workplace is not individually tailored. Nobody's ever asked me what I'm good at; nor am I often asked what things I want to work on—that's only happened twice. I find my work assignments rarely require any type of higher intellect or skills;

getting into "flow" is difficult when the work isn't motivating. Practicing positivity is tough in this bland corporate environment where everybody is just plugging away at their computer, and I don't think there's a single living plant in my building, so the environment isn't very uplifting.

Part of why I don't feel very included in my work group is because I never really know what's going on around me. Things are happening, but I'm not in the loop on it, which is too bad because it would be a great learning experience. When I ask what's going on, I get a really brief explanation, but the attitude and culture here is that everybody needs to just focus on getting their own work done, so it feels intrusive to ask about that stuff, and people don't feel super open to it. I do feel like I can't be myself in certain ways because the expectation here is that everybody will do engineering forever, but that's not how I feel. Keeping career goals close to the chest is probably fairly common in workplaces though.

Boeing's a great company, and the products are awesome, so that part works, but personally I don't take pride in my work or the fact that I work for Boeing. Mostly it's a financial transaction in exchange for my time—it's like a job versus a career. It feels like because we're paid so much from the union contracts, our work doesn't need to be appreciated, which is totally backwards, but oh well. After realizing I was unhappy in my job, I decided to be proactive and learn as much as I could about why that may be and what I can do about it. I've found I can probably treat the symptoms of an unfulfilling job, but my research points to the conclusion that the problems are pretty fundamental to Boeing—so I'm trying to break my golden handcuffs and [am] looking outside the company for a new career. A lot of the problems are more or less symptoms of a gigantic, publicly traded manufacturing company. One person has little impact; the focus is exclusively on profits; the company value is in product data and processes, not on employee talent. But that's no excuse, and the company will continue to suffer in the job marketplace.

MEL MYER

When people ask me now how I like working at Boeing, I say that I hated it, that the work was very tedious and very monotonous. [. . .] I don't have too many positive things to say. I tend to, you know, mention the nice people I've met. But in terms of the working culture, I'm really glad to be leaving.

—Stress analyst, age thirty, two years at Boeing,
interviewed in 2013

I started at Boeing Commercial in the summer of 2011 as a stress analyst. I've actually wanted to work at Boeing for a long time, since college. I had worked at another company before Boeing, and while there I applied to see if I could move up to Seattle and work there. I came in really motivated and excited. When I started it was probably similar to any other large company where there wasn't any sort of training period or clear direction that was ever given to me. Even on my first day, my boss had not told me where to go. I was sitting in the lobby trying to find where my cubicle and my group were. I guess that was all kind of a preview of what's to come. My boss finally got in touch with me and told me where to go and meet my group after waiting for like forty-five minutes or so. It is a stressful time when you start a brand-new job after you move across the country. So, a little bit of a surprise that they didn't say, "Hey! Welcome!"

The first two months, there wasn't too much to do. My leader was a very old-school guy. He was probably in his early fifties. And he was the one who was supposed to be mentoring me and directing me in my day-to-day activities. But he just gave me very open-ended direction: "Okay, just read this" or "There's a bunch of files in that folder. Just look through them and understand them." So I was on my own until work started coming in, and even then it wasn't very clearly defined. I was a little frustrated that I didn't have someone explain the process of what was going on or someone to really check up on me. Even though I sat next to my lead, he did very little to help me develop in terms of getting me suggestions or training to take or people to talk to or other helpful things. Of course, there is some expectation that you are going to take some initiative and do some things on your own. But I think you can develop so much faster if there was someone who was pointing you in the right direction.

From what I've heard, that's the old Boeing culture: I do my work; you do yours. Work on your own; do your own thing. When I asked him if I can talk to other groups to have them show me something, he'd say, "No, you're in this group. Only talk to these few people. Everyone else has their own thing to do. Don't bother them." Boeing recognizes this is a problem and is trying to fix it. But I think it mostly is just the older people who have spent thirty or forty years in an aerospace career.

All I really saw was management focused on meeting deadlines and arbitrary dates. They didn't really care how you got there. I didn't see senior management, but I think they knew all the problems. They set up Facebook for young engineers to know each other, and they also set up a mentor thing, education and training opportunities. I saw lots of things upper management was doing. But because it was a cultural problem, all the people in the middle were still in the old Boeing culture, so there wasn't too much they could do to fix it. The first thing I would do as a manager is really get actively involved with young people when they start. Really make actual progressions about what they'd like to do to help their career and, maybe at the one-year mark, meet with them and say, "Here's three other opportunities in the company you should go to if you want." Really make it easy to move around and find what they like. That really lets people adjust to their job roles or the program. I think if people stay in the same group and can't get out, they might feel like they're stuck, and quitting is the only way to get out of it.

When people ask me now how I like working at Boeing, I say that I hated it, that the work was very tedious and very monotonous. I didn't see management going out of their way to recognize what new employees are interested in. I just have a very cynical view now of the company based on my experiences and views of the structure. I don't have too many positive things to say. I tend to, you know, mention the nice people I've met. But in terms of the working culture, I'm really glad to be leaving. I'm going back to the employer I worked for, doing mostly consulting work.

What drove me back to that company was the variety of work. At Boeing I just had my small team, and we just worked on the same thing day in and day out. You weren't doing much engineering in terms of solving open-ended problems and really designing and changing things—very compartmentalized—and we had very little authority or opportunity to change anything. With my new employer, I'll work on a project, maybe two projects at the same time in completely different industries. You don't get bored very easily. Whereas at Boeing, after a couple of months, it was the same kind of business, so it was boring.

The other thing is recognition. I got "Thanks" and "You did a really good job," but the recognition I was used to was if you did a good job on something, it meant you getting involved in meetings with higher-ups or my boss will send an e-mail to the vice president of the company. For Boeing, there wasn't much of that. I was just a very small cog in a giant machine. Management was always busy, and if I did a good job, I was just assigned an even more tedious amount of work, nothing really stimulating. So you learn that if I really do a good job that just means that I get more work. That demotivates you and slowly makes you put less of an effort into your work. In contrast, at my previous employer, if I was seeking out additional paths or doing a good job at something, he would find things for me to do. That gave me ownership or some authority. I felt like I wasn't just spending my entire ten years doing one thing, so to speak.

It's pretty terrible to say, but many of the engineers were demoralized, and the expectations for them were very low. At Boeing, people worked at a much slower pace, and there wasn't much of an urgency to do things more efficiently. I read a book on that, the lazy culture. Here's an example. I wrote a large report that was previously done by four or five people by just working two or three hours a day and the rest of the time I would just surf the Internet, drink coffee, walk around the buildings. After six months, I rewrote the entire thing to make it easier to read, put in the numbers, sent it out, and the manager gave me an "exceeds expectations" on my performance review. That got me thinking, me putting in 40 percent effort got me an "exceeds expectations." I am not a lazy person. I would rather be busy all day. That was just really eye-opening to me.

I was pretty proud that I worked at Boeing on the 747. At the end it was just like, "I don't really care that I work at Boeing." Or when the issues with the 787 were going on, we all knew it wasn't a major safety event; it would just look really bad, but it wasn't going to be an injury to people. We just saw that as trouble: it was going to cost Boeing a lot of money. Other people just really didn't care about it. That isn't to say that we didn't care about it being done correctly, which is something positive about Boeing. Boeing engineers want to make sure that everything is safe and that it's not going to be an issue on the airplane.

One of my major reasons for leaving is that I don't think Boeing is a good long-term investment. Boeing is trying to move jobs out of Puget

Sound. I wasn't confident that I would have a job in twenty or thirty years. People who are tied to the company for twenty or thirty years will have to move across the country or have to quit a job they like. That's going to be a problem. I think the company is probably going to get in some trouble in the next ten years or so with the union and the slow pace of work and the management mentalities and the high cost of labor and the outsourcing of work to other parts of the country. I'm really glad that I got away. I'm interested to see how it pans out, to see if I'm right, if Boeing goes down the tube. I want to see what the turnover of young engineers will be. For people who are motivated and ambitious, Boeing is not a good place. If the young and ambitious leave, you just have the leftover work culture of people who don't change things.

I'd much rather find jobs that I enjoy and find challenging and stimulating than just a paycheck. So happiness is a goal. Boeing is probably one of the best places I can work for guaranteed raises and bonuses and pensions. But I gave that up for my old company without guaranteed bonus and raises and no good benefits because I know I will be happy even though I may not get paid as much. I'll enjoy my hours at work and not hate my job. I think the young engineers are happy there. So they must be doing something right.

In the grand scheme of things, I didn't really have an impact on anything at Boeing. I was just a very small part in the giant machine. I want to work on projects from start to finish, building an actual article, actually have impact in terms of what my analysis was and how it was used in each of the designs. I want to be known as someone who was a good supervisor, leader, manager. Like someone who helps develop engineers, and people say, "Yeah, I'm glad I work for him because he really helped me with my career and to be a better engineer."

GERRY FRITZ

There is quite a disconnect between management and employees. It seems like the management is all about stock prices and their investors.

—Engineer, approximately twenty-two years old, four months
at Boeing, interviewed in 2012

I am a design engineer in the mechanical hydraulics group on the 747. Honestly, I do not know how many positions I applied to at Boeing. It was over thirty. Anything in engineering level one or two, in mechanical/structural, I applied to it, and this is the only one where I got past the electronic screening of my resume and got hired. I feel pretty damn lucky. I've never been paid anywhere remotely close to this. I was very happy with the pay. Benefits, I had no idea, but from what everyone is saying, the benefits package is excellent. I have no contributions whatsoever, so everything is covered. I am very happy with that side.

I had such an outside perspective: you see the face of Boeing from the outside, and now, part of it is definitely different. I had friends who had internships with Boeing and friends who also had parents that worked for Boeing. You know, you don't get an accurate portrayal from other people. Well, it is simply different from what I expected. It's the Boeing way that everything takes a long time. It is very bureaucratic; it is such a big company; everything takes so long for anything to go anywhere. It is just slow. I guess "inefficient" is another word that comes to mind. A lot of it is also the old-timers. Don't take offense here, but people who have been working here for twenty years, that is what they are used to, so they have become complacent. You know, it is the Boeing way.

To be honest, I thought that I would jump right in, and everyone at Boeing would work really hard. I didn't realize how much time people wasted. I have been training almost four months now, and I feel like I haven't done anything; I haven't learned nearly as much as I was expecting. I've had one little project where I had to move a hydraulic 2.2 inches: that is what I have to show for four months at the Boeing Company. I was expecting a closer-knit environment, even within my own working group. I am the youngest person in my group by I think about eight years or so, so that's not bad. No one goes for a drink after work. I guess a couple times a year there is a party, like a Christmas party, but overall it's not too bad really.

There is a lot of butting heads between groups. No one can communicate effectively, except for the managers. What I've noticed is the higher up the manager, the less they say in more words. Generally I'd say people don't like change. Say there is a drawing and they have been doing the drawing the same way for fifteen years, and someone from a different group, who they already don't like, says they have to change it. Even if that person is right, they are extremely resistant to it.

You see people that stand around and talk. I do it. There have been days I talked to the lady next to me for two hours over the course of the day. That, and coming in right when the new contract [was agreed], you kind of see the ugly side of that. It's pretty prevalent, all these things I am saying. And a lot of it is what I have learned from people, maybe not what I have seen firsthand or maybe a little bit of what I have seen firsthand, but that fits right in with what other people have been saying. I saw some of my friends this weekend, and, you know, we are complaining about software and training, complaining about the database crashing, and it is like, "Yeah, we have the same thing here; we have this version of it. They created some shortcut that automatically closes down the program. It is that bad that they created something to shut down the program; they didn't fix it." So it seems pretty widespread with other new employees I know also.

Training is terrible. You sit in a classroom for eight hours a day, and you try to learn, and your brain gets overloaded. It sucks and is kind of a waste of time. Compared to school the material is very easy, and it is a very mixed classroom; I'm with people who have been at Boeing thirty years, me a few months. I'm with people who are waiting to retire in a few years. Not to brag, but I feel like I am, you know, maybe if not smarter, at least I am more receptive to that type of environment because I have been going through it my entire life. I would say that I am pretty smart, and I pick stuff up quickly, and unfortunately because of that, I can be pretty lazy too. It is like, slow down, like, you have a lecture and then you have an exercise to do, and they tell you exactly what to do step by step, like, "No, click here, and then click here, and then click here," and it takes me five minutes but twenty minutes for the class to finish. But, at the same time, they are paying me over $60,000 a year to sit on my ass, really. So as much as I want to complain, I don't feel like I really can or I should.

Generally I think that SPEEA is just overkill. Just being thrown into the whole negotiation thing—I don't really know what to think. You have Boeing saying, "We need to cut costs, blah blah blah." And SPEEA is saying, "Management is trying to screw you over." You can't believe either side, but at the same time they both have relevant points. Except they have taken it too far. SPEEA . . . I do feel they have a small important function of maintaining a reasonable salary level or contract because I know management would try to chop that down if SPEEA wasn't there to fight, but at the same time they are asking for too much; they want a 6 percent wage pool in the current contract, and of course that is not going to happen. It is like they are trying to force us to strike; you get both sides, but I don't think either have the employees' best interests in mind. Honestly, I don't know what to believe.

There is quite a disconnect between management and employees. It seems like the management is all about stock prices and their investors. Really it is. For example, the whole '87 program is just the marvel of the jet age. But it was 3.5 years late; it cost billions of dollars extra; management decided to try a whole new method. They outsourced the wings to Japan. Formerly, the wings were Boeing's pride and joy, and they sent them off. They tried this whole new cost-saving thing, and it just backfired in their face, and then they want to give us less benefits and lower the wage pools. It just seems like they are disconnected. Seems like they are not doing what is best for the company and best for the employees. It feels like employees don't feel as valued. But at the same time, people don't work very hard, or they don't have to work very hard.

Boeing does not make me inclined to be that invested in my position. We just do hydraulic tubing. I do not want to just be designing hydraulic tubing the rest of my life—that sounds awful and extremely boring. It is a means to an end. Through this position I will be able to transfer to something I will enjoy a lot more. I can't do that right now because I am new and being cautious. I don't want to jump in and be like, "Oh, thanks for hiring me. I am going to transfer to a different group." I do value creativity and enjoy problem solving and not doing the same thing day in day out. I know the Boeing Company is so big that everyone has to specialize, but over time I would like to go into fluid dynamics, something like that. In the meantime I will get paid a lot for not doing much at all.

I really don't know [if I will stay at Boeing for my career]. On one side it is very comfortable; I get paid well, excellent benefits, and there is a chance I could move all around the country. If I wanted to move to another program, they will pay for an MA degree, and I could easily go into management. But at the same time, I don't know how satisfying it would be. It is one thing to be comfortable but another thing to actually enjoy what you are doing. It is four months of my career, and I just don't know. What I am trying to do now is build a foundation, and then we will see. Maybe I will go to another company. I have thought about doing Engineers without Borders. Just see what happens.

11

ACCEPTING THE NEW REALITY

On the face of it, the voices from the four employees in this chapter seem to describe reasonably happy and productive work lives. Although it took one young woman two job transfers before she finally found a satisfactory niche, these employees are united by the fact that their day-to-day Boeing existence—the tasks and/or the people with whom they work—is agreeable. They are able to be creative and innovative, to solve interesting problems, or to make useful contributions to the group. Often they mention that they have been recognized for a job well done, and the impact of their work, even if small or in its infancy, seems to be an important source of satisfaction. And when this satisfaction begins to wane, as in the case of one employee we interviewed here, they are motivated to seek a transfer within the company. Work in which they can be engaged and involved is an important driver.

But compared to other employees we have encountered to this point, this group of young, newly hired workers differs in some important ways. Even more so than other employees, they seem to have a greater degree of acceptance regarding Boeing's corporate ethos. This is not to say that all *approve* of these values (indeed, one is frustrated that he cannot get a pay raise because of corporate "penny pinching"), but there does appear to be a frank recognition that these simply *are* the company's values. They acknowledge, for example, that the company is shareholder driven and may not stay in the Puget Sound region; they recognize that pensions are a thing of the past and no longer have the expectation that Boeing, or any company for that matter, will provide such financial security. And while they may point to problems connected to such strategies—to be sure, they are often very critical, as we have seen in other chapters—they seem less concerned with and occasionally even embrace this new philosophy. One young woman remarks about the prospect of Boeing leaving the Puget Sound region, "I would actually be okay with it because I would just go back to school." Another notes matter-of-factly that he suspected the company's concern with safety was "purely stockholder driven," and a third plainly summed up his perspective by remarking, "No one wants to work for a company that doesn't want to make money."

We also see a shift in thinking regarding two concepts that have been historically important to the commitment levels of Boeing employees: the Boeing name and the prospect of long-term job security. For these new hires, the company name does not connote such a uniformly positive reaction. Pride in working for the Boeing family seems to have been replaced with pride in one's own high-quality work. Throughout the interviews one does not sense that these employees have ever been as emotionally connected to or enamored with the Boeing name (even though some like the prestige they get when others hear that they work for the company). In fact, two mention how their images of the company conjured up notions of a stagnant and dull career, one that they did not necessarily desire.

Regarding job security, two employees observe that the company does not seem to actively entice newly hired employees to stay with the company, and two adopt what some might consider a callous attitude toward the concept of long-term employment. One notes how companies need to "cull the herd" on occasion, and another points out that "valuable workers" do not need to fear layoffs. They will be retained based on their own merit, which they, themselves, have cultivated. These brave positions reveal that these younger workers simply have little expectation that companies value or will be loyal to their workers over time.

Alongside this more detached stance toward "corporate Boeing" is a strong belief in a "do-it-yourself" narrative and in the power of one's own "can-do" spirit. Although several workers stress the importance of good mentoring and supportive supervision, they are also quick to mention that opportunities are present for people who take them and leverage what the company has to offer. Mentoring has been helpful to them because they, unlike other employees, have taken advantage of the help. They have carved out their own destinies. As a group they seem to possess a strong belief in the principle of merit: that people both earn and should earn what they get. We see evidence of this view in some of their remarks about unions: that unions make workers lazy because of the unmerited protection they offer, that unions are "whiney" and secure benefits for workers that they probably could achieve on their own. Comments one worker who concedes that the union question is complex, "I don't really know. I haven't seen anyone who is really bullied by the company that didn't do something that deserved it."

Clearly, these attitudes are not held by all newly hired workers. They do, however, constitute a decided shift from what we saw among older retired and still employed workers—a shift in perspective that more readily accepts Boeing's changed organizational character, is less emotionally attached to the Boeing name and corporate pride, and emphasizes the role of employee responsibility for job and career outcomes.

MIKE DEVANT

> From a job security standpoint, I was under the impression that, other than the ten-, twenty-thousand-person layoffs, that any given job is pretty secure compared to the total number. You kinda need to cull the herd every once in a while.
>
> —Equipment assembly designer, age twenty-nine, two years
> at Boeing, interviewed in 2013

I am an equipment assembly designer and design robots to form an assembly-line operation. Before, I worked at a Boeing supplier for similar products. I was expecting there to be less work pressure at Boeing. I was expecting to outshine peers easier at Boeing. I found that to be true to some degree but not as much as expected.

There are a lot of very smart people in Boeing, but there's also poor use of the engineering and intelligence of the employees. They're using people that are very smart for something that they are not smart at. There's a career progression where you are expected to deliver more and are paid more professionally, and suddenly it comes to a point where you supervise people even though supervising people may not be what you're strong at. There's no track that allows you to continue to be smart and come up with cool things—where you can be a good inventor if that's what you're good at.

I would like to be able to come up with ideas, and then go into the shop and help put them together, and then try to vision that out to the factory. That's pretty much what I do right now, and so I am pretty free. I can see being able to do that every single day from nine to five for twenty, twenty-five years—that's another seventeen years from now. I don't know if there's anywhere to go from there. That's basically the current path I'm on. Right now, I love what I do. I'm really enjoying myself. I'm in my home. When I generate something cool, I fire up a patent application. And every time that's happened, I've gotten a check for $450. The opportunity to create exists for everyone, but I don't think they are utilized at all. They're wildly underutilized.

I had no expectations of a pension, and I am glad that I did mine before the most recent agreement. It's nice to have a defined benefit in addition to my 401(k). It was a pleasant surprise because I didn't think anyone did that anymore. From a compensation and benefit package, I am pretty damn well compensated. I have taken three development classes per year and at least six outside courses. So I get to take off Tuesday and Wednesday nights and get paid by the company to take the class. The only problem I'd ever have is the gas to get there. From a job-security standpoint, I was under the impression that other than the ten-, twenty-thousand-person layoffs, that any given job is pretty secure compared to the total number. You kinda need to cull the herd every once in a while.

It's hard to put my finger on a company-wide personality because it's such a big company. You can walk into something that's going to fulfill your dreams. You're welcome to do that. It's pretty easy to do that. It's a true job adventure of a company. You can be whatever you want to be, believe whatever you want. But it's also really easy to disappear. You can walk into it like a cog, a little tiny gear in a machine.

The company is trying to push some of the wrong values down from the top. You know, they're driving for cost and efficiency, and around the middle of new management, it gets lost. The individual managers tend to push higher production. But if you are constantly, insanely driving all the people below you, then you wear them out, and they just don't care anymore. You bring in a new guy, and he's going to learn that he should just do his time and go home. It's more societal than anything else. I'm not a big fan of this US workforce at the moment.

In my group, 50 percent of them are within five years of retirement, and there is this ten-year experience gap where nobody was hired. That's gonna hit in the next five to ten years when those people retire, and there's not going to be anyone on the upper end of the scale. There's a bunch of programs to help new engineers with mentors, but it doesn't seem like a whole lot of mentorship comes out of that—there's not actually a lot of transferring of knowledge. There's no, "Hey, you guys are going to have the same job function. Why don't you work with him and see what they do and do that?" It's more of, "Hey. We'll meet up once a month and have coffee together and talk about what you're doing."

Generally, in a union there's too much posturing, too much politics for my taste. I understand the point of a union. I'm not generally pro-union. I think they've gotten greedy, and their threat of strikes has been tremendously damaging. If you go and look at the South Carolina factory, their employees are paid less, so it makes sense for Boeing to do work there, which argues for the free market. There's a place that people can get really bullied by their company (sighs). I don't really know. I haven't seen anyone who is really bullied by the company that didn't do something that deserved it. I hope they [the unions] cease to be in power. [. . .] Because if they don't give over some of the power, the price is the mechanics and engineers are out of a job.

I identify more with the engineer/inventor identification than the Boeing identification. I feel like there's some baggage that's tied along with "Oh, I'm an engineer at Boeing" in this Seattle area. Everyone has an engineer in their family. You know, it's the dad, the uncle; it's the brother . . . Everyone has an engineer something. A lot of times it's kind of this black box that people go into, and they work thirty-five years, and then they retire.

I am happy to work for Boeing and pleased to tell people that I work for Boeing because there are a lot of people that want to work for Boeing. I am very proud of the job I do. I'm proud of what I produce. I am much more fulfilled with my work than I feel I should be, if that makes sense. There's an expectation in American society where I go to work because I have to. I don't feel like that. I go to work because I like what I do. I enjoy it. I love my wife. I love my kids. I have a great time with them. But sometimes I get tired of that and work—it's very stressful at times, but it's definitely a net positive. If I were not doing something that I enjoyed, I don't think I could do it for very long.

My work does make a difference, but a small difference. I mean it's so big, like a giant river. If I'm a little squirt gun in the middle of the river squirting at the bank, I can maybe roll a little bit in the bank, and technically that's changing the direction of the river. But I'm not going to take the whole thing and move it. I'll just move it over an inch. I can add something to the entire system, but sometimes it gets overwritten by people who yell louder than I do—people that use a whole bunch of jargon, shouting, "Synergy, harmonize, reinvent the paradigm" (laughs). Those things get the attention of people who are up the food chain. Those are the ones who actually define what the paradigm is.

KEITH DEVINE

> The people I work with are great—friendly, willing to work with you.
> Everyone's happy; we're a great team. . . . But the corporate aspect
> of the company . . . I'm a bit pessimistic towards the corporation.
> —Engineer, age twenty-nine, two years at Boeing,
> interviewed in 2013

Honestly, why I chose Boeing—it's a large company, it's a little more stable than a smaller company, and the pay was better than where I was at. I was at a smaller company that was known to hire fresh out-of-college grads and pay them bare bones but give them good experience. You are salaried, and there's no union: you get paid for forty hours, but you work sixty, and they expect you to put in sixty-five. I was kind of tired of being overworked and underpaid.

My first day was an orientation for at least a couple hundred of us. It was pretty cool—basically try to get you jazzed up. You're working for the biggest aerospace company in the world, so that's pretty cool. When I reported to work, they didn't seem totally prepared for me. Probably two or three days later, they sent me off to what's called "M-E academy," which is manufacturing engineering academy. It's basically two months of "This is how you become a manufacturing engineer." After two months I came back to my business unit, and it was still almost like

I didn't even leave. They were still kind of, "Okay, what are we going to have him do?"

So I just started attending as many meetings as I could to get people's names, faces, the products I'd be working on, and kind of shadowing other engineers that have my job to understand what's going on. I followed my team lead around, asking a lot of questions, and he was the person I shadowed, and when he was busy, I would be helped by the senior process engineer that was sitting right next to me. Between the two of them and my manager, they pretty much answered all my questions, kept my time as full as possible. In all honesty, it wasn't very long after I got back from the M-E before I was running my own meetings, and I hit the ground running. It wasn't a lot of pressure. It was like, "That's okay. You're a young engineer, and you've seen things. We know you're going to learn as you go, but this is what you'll be doing, so give it a try," so it wasn't too scary. It wasn't long after that I was given a special project. The managers thought I could handle it; it would be a good challenge, a good advance for me. I have plenty of friends in the company that are in other MBUs, and they're just like, "Wow, you're really lucky; there's nothing like that going on around here." So, yeah, I think I make a difference. I've implemented some things that, even as a lowly two-year engineer, have saved the company tens of thousands, if not more, in some little products we've got going on, so that's cool.

The people I work with are great—friendly, willing to work with you. Everyone's happy; we're a great team; we all get along—it's great. In my particular location, it wasn't so much pressure to perform; it's just, "Do your best; that's what we expect of you, but we understand you're going to fall and stumble every once in a while and learn from those mistakes." But the corporate aspect of the company, especially just coming out of negotiations with the union not too long ago, I'm a bit pessimistic towards the corporation. Obviously, they stopped pensions for new hires. That's a big loss. And with such record profits, after the negotiations we felt more like worker bees, just commodities. There's still that feeling of "Wow, we're getting screwed, and we're going to have to take what we can get because the company's hell bent on taking all they can get and having record profits."

I don't know what they're doing with it all. I would assume they're developing the next couple of plane programs they're working on. That's what we all tell ourselves, but when you hear about these billions of dollars, you're just like, "But where is that going?" Then you hear about these executives' bonuses that are just outlandish—you gotta wonder. It's like, "They're not really leading by example. Hey, he gets, you know, a $10 million bonus; why don't we get at least market bonus standards?" Why are they not giving us the industry standard if we're the best employees in the world, the best engineering staff?

During negotiations, we have meetings both with the union staff and Boeing. I did a lot of reading because you have two completely polarized sides. You have corporate, and they're going to want to maximize shareholder value. They even told us that's one of their top three goals. And then you have the union, which is, "We want the most for our employees no matter what." But we got to have a happy medium, and so, you know, there's spin. We were getting e-mails from the union and e-mails from corporate within five minutes to half an hour of each other; it was crazy. They would have rebuttals ready. It was weird, because some of the e-mails we got were almost childish. I remember—I think Mike Delaney sent one out—it was like, "Really? Really? You're a world-class executive, and you let your emotions show through the e-mail that much? It's about holding your emotions, buddy."

If we didn't have a union, then I would imagine it would be much worse. I don't think a big company our size would really go out of their way to make sure we have exceptional benefits unless someone held them accountable, because they're so profit driven at this size, margins are tighter, and they're trying to invest in R&D and everything. And they have shareholder value to worry about, which I think is BS. We should be about the quality of the planes and our name and reputation in the industry. The economy is bouncing back, but we're not seeing our salaries bounce back with it. They're still not hiring like they used to. It's just like, "Why is the economy getting better, and we all hurt?" The companies clearly don't care, so somebody's got to hold them accountable. I don't see any other way because they don't hold themselves accountable.

It's kind of sad because the old Boeing way used to be, "Come and have a career for life." They say that our generation bounces from company to company, and so they're not going to try to really retain us like they would in the past—they're just going to give us a 401(k) that's transferrable between companies instead of the pension. They've not really given any sort of incentives to stay with the company. Nothing has been said, like, "We invest hundreds of thousands of dollars in training and schooling and software, and we'd like to try to keep you here as both an investment in your career and investment in our company and progress." There are plenty of people that, like myself, would love to stay with the company for life. It's a little disheartening to see they're not trying to keep us loyal, keep us at the company. They just say, "Oh, yeah, it's a fact of nature. You're probably going to leave so, that's the way it is."

So, yeah, I work with pride, working for the biggest aerospace company in the world. The local culture's great; it's a really good place to work. The corporate culture could be better and less focused on shareholder value and more on building the best plane and rewarding employees for their good hard work. It would be nice if they had incentives for staying with the company for a long time, try to encourage people to have a career that's for life, and "We'd really prefer it, so here's a carrot if you're willing to stick around."

CATHY ALLWOOD

> What surprises me—they're supposed to be cutting-edge, but they just recycle so much. They took the 737 that's currently flying, and they just put on new engines and call it a new airplane. So that's what I struggle with. I mean, yeah, they're going to make a lot of money off of it, but in terms of my job, it makes it a lot less interesting.
> —Technical designer, age twenty, one year at Boeing,
> interviewed in 2013

Growing up here, I always knew Boeing was a place where people worked for forty years and all the people were old (laughs)—my perception of it. I actually did not want to work for Boeing when I first started. I wasn't really interested in airplanes; I just liked the money aspect of it (laughs). My grandpa worked for Boeing in, like, World War II, and I just knew church people or people in the community who worked for Boeing. I always knew people worked for Boeing for thirty, forty years who are looking for that kind of stability, so I guess that's wise. The fact that it's so stable turned me off from it.

I've been working for Boeing for almost two years, and I'd say now I've found a group that I can be happy in finally after three tries. It sounds silly, but simple things like I have a window now, and the people I work with are amazing compared to where I was in Everett. Every morning my current lead comes in and says, "Good morning. How are you doing today?" I've never had a lead do that; usually they just kind of grimace, "Morning"—usually have to force it out of them. That's the great thing about my lead; he's kind of a people person. The first day he just let me know his expectations for me—like, we expect you to ask questions; don't sit and fake it. Any questions, he's overly helpful; he'll send me links to whatever I need, and we talk things out, and he's encouraging—actually the first time I've ever really gotten encouragement.

Now that I'm in Renton with this group, I can actually see myself staying for a little longer. And being such a small group, I actually feel like I'm contributing quite a bit. I think the biggest thing that changed my outlook and my expectations was seeing myself have a spot in the group, like a contributing role. And it helps to feel like you're on the same playing field. It's like I'm an equal with everyone, and they respect my opinion, and they listen to me, and that alone is a big thing. I've become friends with them. We play beach volleyball in the park during lunch, and everyone joins in like it doesn't matter what age. It's pretty awesome.

I've heard after five years you've been brainwashed (laughs). I don't know if it's true—I heard it from an HR person at another company. I heard it from Microsoft people that after five years at Boeing, certain companies will just throw your resume in the trash. Yeah, it's kind of mind-boggling because Boeing people become really set in their ways. I don't know, you can't think for yourself, and then I guess the new employers just get tired of hearing, "Well, that's not how Boeing did it." I am worried that if, at the five-year mark, my brain chemistry changes, and you're no longer a creative individual. But this new group has kind of changed my perspective on things—don't seem quite so depressed (laughs). I mean, my lead has probably been there twenty years, but he still acts like a little kid. It's good that he has a sense of humor; he's useful, sharp, so maybe it's not really true. But I don't want to risk it (laughs).

The company-wide values don't really influence me that much; it's kind of something you have to sit in like once a year. Basically common sense, like everything that they promote company-wide is just things that you would probably normally do if you had decency—like "One Boeing Way." How about, "Let's not talk bad about your coworkers?" Or maybe, "You should work together with your coworkers." Kind of all Care Bears stuff. [. . .] It's very possible that people don't have common sense.

The one thing that does seem to influence layoffs is all the talk of not making the Seattle area an epicenter for engineering anymore. Not a completely new idea, but they've announced it more frequently recently. I would actually be okay with it because I would just go back to school (laughs). Yeah, I mean, I'm not looking to stay at Boeing for more than, well, after I get my bachelor's I'm not going to be at Boeing anymore. That's the plan, so, no more than next three years from now.

The culture? Oh yeah, well, the stingy parts surprised me quite a bit. They value innovation, but then they value stinginess. I don't think those things can always exist together. Like, they'll just reuse things so much, and it kind of takes away the fun out of my job because I'm supposed to be designing things, but they just use the same design that they've had for twenty years because they work and then just make my job paperwork. That's actually the main reason why I don't see myself staying for very long. We don't get to do anything original, almost hardly ever. Everything's about saving costs, but there really isn't that much creativity. . . . You could get creative for how you interpret policies (laughs). Yeah, creatively interpret standards and three-hundred-page documents about things you don't care about. Occasionally I'll get to take points for where I want piping to run through the plane, and there's slight freedom in that, but I did it when I first started in this group, then I realized, "Oh, that's it. That'll be it for a while." What surprises me—they're supposed to be cutting-edge, but they just recycle so much. They took the 737 that's currently flying, and they just put on new engines and call it a new airplane. So that's what I struggle with. I mean, yeah, they're going to make a lot of money off of it, but in terms of my job, it makes it a lot less interesting.

At first I didn't know what the union was about—I still don't know exactly—but I went to an informational session right before the negotiations. People were really friendly, but they seemed like they had such an agenda. I started to get suspicious just because they seemed so outraged and so inflammatory; it seemed a little over-the-top to me at first. If they could just tone it down a bit—like, give the facts and then they can go scream and yell later—that'd be good. I find myself looking for a middle ground with the media. I mean, I never thought I'd go looking at news articles—figure out what is actually true. I'm skeptical of Boeing too. Of course, businesspeople are going to cut costs and stuff, so there's some truth to SPEEA's objections to the contracts, like when they rejected it. I actually did march with a couple of coworkers, and it was an interesting experience. I think we were doing it for the cultural experience. I don't know, it's kind of fun to join a little movement. It gets the blood running through your veins (laughs). It's kind of like once in a lifetime, so I guess that's why I was doing it (laughs), but whether or not I really thought that SPEEA was making a difference, I don't know about that. All my coworkers just seem so flippant about it. They didn't seem to give SPEEA any attention—just wait till this blows over so we can get back to work. SPEEA did strike me as a bit whiney. I still don't know what they do (laughs). I think they negotiated, and then we just basically picked up the same contract, which was per our vote, I suppose, but I don't know how much power they have.

I don't feel like my job is using my skills and my interests very well, so it's not really a huge part of who I am. Everything I learned in school vaguely applies to my job. Most of what I've learned is on the job and common sense. I don't derive a lot of purpose from my job because I am trying to find what I want to do and what I like doing. I try to find meaning in other areas of my life.

WES BARTLETT

> No one wants to work for a company that doesn't want to make money.
>> —Stress analyst, age twenty-eight, eleven months at Boeing,
>>> interviewed in 2013

After working at essentially a smaller version of Boeing, I wanted to work at a larger company that was more stable. I hired into Boeing as a stress analyst, and I was excited about the work I was going to be doing. I guess I kind of assumed everyone else there would also be excited and proud of what they work on and would be diligent workers. I am now working on the program side: my job is to analyze the plane to make sure that it's not going to break when it's flying through the sky or, more recently, that it will survive a crash landing. One of the issues I ran into with a smaller company was that it was harder to move up, not necessarily that it was harder to be recognized and seen as a valuable component to the company. But it was more of, "Well, there's only one person that's above you, so until he's leaving, retires, quits, or dies, you're going to have to stay where you're at." So I like that Boeing offers multiple opportunities. I feel like I can really thrive here, not necessarily here being in Puget Sound but here within the company. Within the company, I don't think that specifically I will ever take credit for any of the airplanes. If you ever talk to anyone on here that does, then they're crazy (laughs). But I think the work that is done by the people in my group obviously makes a difference.

My work consumes an average of forty hours a week of my life. I would be happy if I got paid a lot of money to work forty hours a week and got to retire at a beach home. I don't let my work really define me unless people ask what I do for a living, but I would be just as happy as a park ranger. In terms of engineering, it's one of the higher-paying career choices one can choose, but that doesn't necessarily have anything to do with Boeing or the work at Boeing. I'm not a big fan of doing lots of overtime. I'm more of the "work to live" not "live to work" kind of people. Actually, I don't really like airplanes except for the fact that they help me fly on vacation, but it really doesn't define me. Usually my friends are not from my work. I usually don't get along very well with engineers outside work: they tend to like to talk about work too much.

It's nice to say that you work for Boeing, mainly because people recognize it, and that was something I wasn't used to before, so that's good. But in terms of what I identify with, I would say, since I've had several jobs already, I identify more with the position than the company. I think that they create a very good product, and they are very good at what they do. And I'd like to think that they actually do hire the best of the best, but I know of a lot of really good engineers that don't work at this company too. But my mom doesn't know that, and that's all that matters!

Whether or not I agree with the union decision, I think that pensions in general are a thing of the past. At my age I feel like I've just missed out. When I've interviewed with companies, I'd get a "Well, we just quit offering pensions" or "There are no pensions," and I always heard, "Why is that? Well, because nowadays people don't stay put very long."

Well, is it because there's no incentive to stay? I understand that it is very expensive to maintain a pension plan, especially for a large work-force. That being said, it was really nice to have, and I wouldn't be surprised if maybe not the next negotiation period or the following, I don't have it, or it gets frozen. So, honestly, I have never acted like I had the pension, and it's never had anything to do with my decision to stay here or to work here. I think Boeing is aware of that fact, and that's why they really pushed hard to get rid of it.

I have a different opinion about job security, I think, than most. I feel that so long as you are efficient at what you do and good at what you do, and so long as you have a company that is managing its money well and can continue to maintain employees, even with small, say, cutbacks or, you know, whatever they call releasing people, firing peo-ple. If you show yourself as a very useful employee of the company, then you usually don't have to worry about layoffs unless they become too severe, so that's another reason why I feel very comfortable at Boeing Commercial. Even if there were to be future cutbacks, I still feel—maybe not so much just because I'm new right now—but if I can stave that off a couple more years, then I feel I'd be in a good position to not have to worry so much. Also, just hard work and getting stuff done in a quick and timely manner—I've gotten more responsibilities, newer responsibility. I've had my managers or my lead say, "Oh, you're doing a really good job. I see a promising future here," those sort of things.

I would be perfectly happy if the union went away tomorrow. I didn't join a fraternity in college because I didn't want to have the decisions of a group represent my decision, and I feel the same way now. While I think that they do mean good and they try and get the best for everybody, I feel that if you work hard enough and if you're unhap-py with the company, you can leave. I think the person that benefits the most is the person that wants to go to work and skate by. They just want to do a little bit of work, but they still want the same promotion that everyone else is going to get. They want the same raise that everyone else is going to get. I look at it the other way around and say, "Well, why do they get the same raise that I would get if I did four things when they did one?" I've worked with people, and they're like, "Oh, I've been at this company for fifteen years, or twenty years," and they carry their little SPEEA Boeing flag, and they're really proud of the union. Some of them are very hard workers, and they're proud of what they do; they take pride in their work and how it's perceived by others. Then there are others: "Oh, I can't do that; I'm going to need more time than that. What are they really expecting of me? They don't understand we're the best in the country right here; they can't get work like this anywhere else." And then they go on and read the news trailer.

Boeing values the interest of their shareholders. You still can see that every decision seems to be based off of the shareholders' best interests. Part of that interest involves maintaining a solid workforce. They value that their employees are happy and that they quote-unquote attract good talent. But in terms of all the decisions that they make, if they really wanted to attract, for example, the best engineers, they would've still kept the pension and used it as a giant advertisement billboard that says, "Hey look, if you're a good engineer come work for us—we have a pension." But that's not a knock against them because if they didn't value their shareholders, they wouldn't have the money to pay for half the stuff that they do, so I understand that; I don't look at it as a bad thing. No one wants to work for a company that doesn't want to make money.

Part IV

Conclusion

12

IMPLICATIONS OF THE NEW SOCIAL CONTRACT

No one can say when the unwinding began—when the coil that held Americans together in its secure and sometimes stifling grip first gave way. . . . The unwinding brings freedom, more than the world has ever granted, and to more kinds of people than ever before— freedom to go away, freedom to return . . . get hired, get fired. . . . This much freedom leaves you on your own. . . . Alone on a land- scape without solid structures, Americans have to improvise their own destinies, plot their own stories and salvations.[1]
—George Packer, *The Unwinding: An Inner History of the New America*, 2013

We assembled this collection of individual stories in the belief that employees deserve a hearing as we seek to understand the transforma- tion of American workplaces. They are, after all, the ones who bear the consequences, both beneficial and harmful, of the many technological, organizational, and cultural changes that are under way. As we have seen, their experiences and responses to the changes are complex and highly personal. To some extent, the particular details and idiosyncratic nature of their responses are the inevitable result of using individual stories to illuminate the experiences of employees through these years of change. If, however, we examine the broader sweep of these stories by combining them into one narrative arc, we can detect an underlying trend in the way the three different cohorts responded to Boeing's transformation. We detect a gradual but unmistakable turn away from the company across time and across generations, evidence perhaps of the larger "unwinding" observed by George Packer. Indeed, the ties that bind employee and employer have become thinner and more frayed as we move further away from Heritage Boeing retirees to those still employed workers who lived through the merger as well as those newly hired by the organization.

The wider economic context and generational shifts in workplace expectations undoubtedly contributed to this weakened connection. But there is little doubt that postmerger Boeing, like many other large companies in the United States, signaled by its actions that it seemed to care less about securing the long-term loyalty and commitment of its employees. As we heard from employees time and again, key developments in this "unwinding," or unraveling, of the postwar social contract included the relocation of Boeing corporate headquarters to Chicago, the opening of a second assembly line in nonunion South Carolina, the move of engineering work overseas or to other locations in the United States, the continued emphasis on shifting design and production of major components of the airplanes to global partners, and the narrowed focus on short-term returns. Taken together, these decisions carried a powerful message: Boeing's commitment to the established workforce and to the Puget Sound region, where the company was founded and where the majority of the work on engineering and assembling commercial airplanes still occurs, was tenuous and contingent. In response, many long-serving employees, with personal experience of Heritage Boeing, disapproved of this new, more distant Boeing, and their emotional connection to the company became more contested and fragile. Younger employees, recently hired and with little direct experience of Heritage Boeing, seemed less resistant to adopting a thinner and more instrumental attachment to the company.

KEY THEMES FROM THE INTERVIEWS

The varied individual stories—each highly nuanced, colorful, and specific to the details of the interviewee's own history—can obfuscate more common patterns and shared reactions. And yet, there were prominent themes that emerged in what the three employee cohorts told us. Among these is how those in the retiree and long-serving currently employed groups remained deeply emotionally connected to Boeing, though their responses to the changes ranged from nostalgia to acceptance to powerful criticism of the postmerger business philosophy and practices. Those with rosy views of Heritage Boeing focused on the quality of the product and the thrill of seeing the planes they worked on take to the sky. They lauded the family feeling, the challenge of the work, and the perceived excellence of the pay, benefits, and opportunities for career advancement. Their emotional attachment had been sustained through the decades and survived the postmerger changes intact. Most were aware of the problems introduced by the new business philosophy but didn't see them as sufficiently damaging to undermine their loyalty to and pride in the company. They still believed that the social contract or exchange between Boeing and them was, on the whole, equitable and balanced.

For other veteran Boeing employees, the problems couldn't easily be swept aside but rather permanently altered how they viewed the company. They believed, with much justification, that Boeing's leaders had badly mishandled the development of the 787 in their efforts to cut costs and minimize risk. Excessive outsourcing and lack of oversight and control of the supply chain on the 787, they felt, were bound to produce serious problems. These employees also regretted what they perceived as Boeing's lack of respect for tribal and tacit knowledge accumulated by the workforce, as well as what they perceived as the company's cavalier attitude toward the preservation and transmission of that knowledge to the new generation of workers. They rued the absence of aerospace experience among top executives and their single-minded pursuit of the bottom line and short-term returns. Especially painful for this group of long-serving employees were the loss of family feeling and the treatment of employees as disposable commodities. For some, this new Boeing cut their emotional ties to the company; for others, it led to a redirection of their emotional investment into the work itself and to ensuring the safety of the product or just taking pride in being a good professional. But whatever the particular employee reaction was to the new Boeing, it was often highly emotional. And as the company's identity changed, employee identities were also affected. Viewed this way, the pervasive, persistent, and strong reaction to company developments is not surprising.

As for the "new hires," the older employees among them are under-standably grateful to have a well-paying job, given the dim prospects for those seeking work in their fifties and sixties, and they play it safe without expressing strong viewpoints. By contrast, many of the younger new hires we interviewed tended to accept Boeing's new business phi-losophy as "normal" or rationalized it as necessary or inevitable in the current tough economic conditions. Profit doesn't seem to be a dirty word for many of them, represented by the frank statement of a young male engineer: "No one wants to work for a company that doesn't want to make money." If they take issue with the corporate philosophy, it is often because they see diminished company innovation contributing to less interesting and creative jobs for them to perform. One of the disil-lusioned newly hired employees told us he was looking to break free of his "golden handcuffs" to find more motivating and meaningful work, blaming the bureaucratic and extreme shareholder-profit-focused cul-ture for his dissatisfaction. By comparison, seasoned Boeing workers more often criticized the changed corporate strategy because they wor-ried about Boeing's long-term capacity to remain viable. Stated one veteran engineer with thirty-three years at the company, "Boeing came from building the best aircrafts, the Cadillacs. A few years ago, Boeing decided that they only had to be good enough; they didn't have to be number one."

The newly hired workers differ from longer-serving employees in other important ways. In two of the new-hire chapters, employees are optimistic about career opportunities; they believe in the power of self-reliance and Boeing as a place where long-term, successful careers are possible, provided they do the necessary legwork. They want the unions to work cooperatively with the company, and where they criticize the unions, it is often because they see them as supporting workers who are undeserving—those who have not earned their way or who do not sub-scribe to the "do-it-yourself" philosophy that often permeates the ranks of younger employees. Such generational differences are corroborated by our 2013 survey data, where we found small but significant genera-tional differences on some measures, with Gen Ys reporting more posi-tive attitudes about Boeing's future and culture, higher levels of organ-izational commitment, and greater perceptions of company support as compared to Gen Xers and baby boomers. Except in the area of pension benefits, Gen Y employees tend to have higher expectations than older workers in terms of development, training, health benefits, and even the provision of services to help with personal problems. Gen Y, however, has higher intent to quit, less job involvement, and the most negative attitudes toward unions.[2] Although the magnitude of the differences is small, they do paint a consistent picture pointing to a gradual but important disengagement of emotion and workplace community despite such generational optimism.

Not all the changes in the Heritage Boeing culture have been considered detrimental. In our previous research, we documented substantial transformations in Boeing's evolution from a male-dominated "good ol' boys" culture to one that was moving, sometimes awkwardly and uncomfortably, toward more equal representation and normalization of women holding jobs that were historically held by men. By most accounts, overt discrimination was a thing of the past, though 2006 survey data pointed to lingering gender differences, with women reporting more disrespectful treatment at work, difficulty fitting into a still male-dominated workplace culture, and perceptions of more critical evaluation of their work performance.

In these most recent narratives,[3] the salience of workplace gender difference seems to have continued to diminish over time. Certainly there are examples in which gender has colored workplace interactions, as when an engineer recalls how she was mistaken for a secretary on her first day of work or when a machinist talks about having to prove herself to male coworkers as possessing enough physical strength to perform the job, while another "flirts" to make "the day go by faster." But it was surprising how infrequently any employee, male or female, mentioned gender as a prominent concern. The 2013 survey data, likewise, corroborate these narratives. On most work-related variables, such as Boeing's culture, general job satisfaction, intent to quit, job involvement, support from the organization, and even work-family conflict, we failed to detect gender differences when looking at all employees across the spectrum of organizational tenure.

Where we did find gender differences, women tended to expect more of the company in the areas of training, job security, and career development; women reported more organizational commitment and more workplace stress; and they said they worked at their full potential a greater amount of the time than did men. They also reported more positive experiences with the unions. Interestingly, though, we also observed a continued narrowing of gender differences whether we cut the data by year of hire or by generational cohort. For example, in 2013, for those hired before 1996, women were some 6 percent higher than men on organizational commitment, but there was virtually no difference between men and women who were hired after 2006. As with other trends we have drawn attention to in these narratives, such change portends a slow, gradual shift, with gender-related differences diminishing rather than widening.

DOES THE CULTURAL SHIFT MATTER?

If the old postwar social contract is gradually being abandoned and supplanted by a more tenuous, instrumental relationship between companies and employees in the United States, as many scholars contend and as our research indicates, the question then becomes, Does it matter, and for whom? Does it matter for companies such as Boeing that worker loyalty and emotional commitment seem to be loosening and becoming frayed? Does it matter that a large segment of the Boeing workforce is disgruntled and no longer enamored with the company? At first glance and by several metrics, the answer for Boeing would seem to be "no" or "not much." With Boeing enjoying record orders far into the future, a stratospheric share price, healthy profits, and continuing and steady increases in productivity,[4] management might feel quite sanguine about reports of worker discontent and disengagement. Moreover, enjoying massive compensation packages, top executives might also feel vindicated in the direction they took, arguing that they deserved such lavish rewards for doing a good job for their shareholders and customers. At first glance, these are powerful arguments that Boeing executives can use to deflect and counter the criticism they receive from labor unions and many of their employees. The company is soaring. Where is the evidence of a problem?

Critics of the company's postmerger policies contend that these good financial results mask underlying dangers that will emerge in the future to endanger the long-term health and vitality of the company. Many point out, for example, that the billions in cost overruns already incurred on the 787 program—overruns that will spread into the future and onto still-to-be-built and delivered airplanes—might seriously jeopardize Boeing's long-term financial health. Only time will tell if Boeing can move quickly enough down the learning curve to start making a profit on the 787 planes it delivers.[5] It can also be argued, as many human resource scholars do, that companies like Boeing lose a great deal of difficult-to-measure benefits in improved innovation, quality, and productivity by not having a fully engaged and empowered workforce. Conclusive evidence in support of such claims is invariably hard to find for a variety of methodological reasons, including the crucial fact that productivity and financial metrics are the result of multiple factors, making it hard to conduct carefully controlled studies.[6] In one sense, Boeing is fortunate as compared to many other large companies in that it produces a product that has a magical aura in the eyes of many employees. As several told us, airplanes are remarkable machines, composed of hundreds of thousands of parts moving in close formation at thirty thousand feet and safely carrying millions of passengers all over the world. Even in this era of exciting technological advances, those who design and build these airplanes can still marvel at the sight of them taking off or flying overhead. This magical quality gives Boeing a unique motivational tool that few other companies possess and mitigates the damaging effects produced by the new corporate culture. Despite this advantage, there is evidence in the survey and narratives that Boeing still operates with a great deal of unused potential work effort.[7]

What of the implications of the changed ethos, culture, and business practices for employees? There have clearly been some deleterious psychological and physical consequences for many employees. Our previous longitudinal research (1997–2006) found that employee attitudes toward top management in particular were severely damaged in the years after the merger, with some two-thirds of employees telling us in 2003 that they did not trust top management. Lost trust is hard to regain, and mistrust seems to linger, as the survey data from 2006 show (with 50 percent still expressing distrust of top management) and as is evident in several of the narratives. We also found that though they started with similar levels of depression and physical symptoms of poor health (for example, headaches, high blood pressure, and back pain), those who remained employed by the postmerger Boeing reported much higher levels of these symptoms than those who left the company after the merger.[8] These are real and measurable effects, and there are solid grounds for attributing them to what was going on at the changed Boeing.

It is also clear that the policies pursued by Boeing since the merger have severely weakened the ability of labor unions to protect their members. In particular, the expanded outsourcing and the actual and threatened location of work outside the Puget Sound region, especially in right-to-work states, as happened with the sending of the second 787 assembly line to South Carolina, have heavily tilted the balance of power toward Boeing and away from the local machinists union (International Association of Machinists and Aerospace Workers [IAM]) and the union that represents engineers and technical workers (Society of Professional Engineering Employees in Aerospace [SPEEA]). As we saw, both the IAM and the SPEEA have had to agree to longer-term contracts (in the IAM case, extending to 2024), meaning that the strike as a negotiating weapon is holstered for many years to come. The contracts also require employees to pay more for health insurance, replace defined benefit pensions with potentially more volatile 401(k) retirement plans, and slow annual salary increases. This decline in union influence at Boeing, long a union stronghold, is, of course, mirrored in the decline in strength in organized labor that is happening across the country, especially in the private sector, where union density and strike activity are at historic lows.[9]

With the leverage afforded companies by globalization and location options for placing work, as well as the pessimism in the workforce about the future effectiveness of unions, particularly among younger employees, what role will unions have in the future? Can labor unions find ways to remain relevant? If they abandon confrontational and power tactics, as some workers recommend, will they have any leverage left at all? Can new forms of worker voice, as exists in Germany with works councils, provide employees with meaningful input into company decisions? We cannot discuss this important issue here,[10] but it seems clear that the traditional avenues by which, in particular, blue-collar workers with less than college educations can achieve middle-class lifestyles are under continued threat. It is hard to think of how such workers can continue to earn a decent living if companies like Boeing continue to squeeze their pay and benefits, introduce more labor-saving technological changes,[11] and relocate work to cheaper locations. To be sure, Boeing's unionized employees are doing quite well today, but they may not do so well in the future as they increasingly confront this new reality on their own.

Finally, the interviews also show that the new Boeing is making it harder for its employees to feel as emotionally invested in and connected to the company as they were in the past. We are not sure if this is necessarily a bad outcome for employees or for civic life. Why isn't it a good thing that employees are not so involved with and beholden to what Lewis Coser calls these "greedy institutions,"[12] that they no longer see these companies as surrogate families that are expected to tend to their emotional as well as material needs? Surely society benefits if workers have a better work-life balance—when they have more time for their families and for civic engagement. What are we to make of the woman we interviewed who admitted she gave her best to the company, and her family got what was left? Is so much lost if workers connect more to their work groups or become invested in the task instead of the company? These questions have no easy answers. What perhaps emerges most clearly in the narratives is that the vast majority of employees need to find some way to attach or invest their emotions at work. Otherwise, they may just go through the motions, as one employee admitted: doing just enough to get by. Moreover, as we have seen, excessive emotional detachment and alienation from work can easily turn into more general cynicism, misery, and disengagement.

Despite the problems, unanswered questions, and uncertainty about the future, we end by highlighting two remarkable characteristics that seem timeless, almost universal, and which survive the ups and downs that inevitably characterize people's work lives. First, the stories illustrate how individuals, regardless of age or attitude to the company, have a powerful desire to find meaning and purpose in their work—to feel that they have made a contribution, however small, to something larger than themselves. Some do it by identifying with the success of their work group or by mentoring young colleagues; others, by seeking to produce safe airplanes for the flying public; and still others, by leveraging their work opportunities into volunteer activities. Second, the stories demonstrate that most workers are remarkably resilient. They are able to adjust to corporate change and the turbulence it produces; they can roll with the punches that are thrown at them and come out whole and, on balance, able to do their work competently. A few embrace the challenges thrown up by the changes and thrive, while some find solace in hanging on to the past. But these stories also show that there are real and damaging consequences when workers believe their leaders have violated norms of trust and respect by privileging the bottom line above all else. We end with the hope that corporate leaders have the good sense to understand that change, while unavoidable and often beneficial, doesn't require the destruction of everything that came before; that efforts to sustain and nourish elements of the old culture that enhance the well-being of all their employees should be as vigorous as those made in the chase for efficiency and better short-term financial results.

APPENDIX

Initially funded by the National Institutes of Health, our ten-year longitudinal panel study (1997–2006) tracked the work attitudes and health of several thousand randomly sampled employees via four comprehensive mail-in surveys and many interviews and focus groups.[1] Following this ten-year study, in 2011, we recontacted those who had previously participated in our research and conducted extensive interviews with many of those who indicated an interest in speaking with us. As would be expected, roughly half were retired, while the others were still employed by the company. A subset of these newly collected interviews from former and current employees comprises the narratives we present in parts I and II.

In the summer of 2013, we conducted another large-scale survey of work attitudes, although this time, thanks to the now widespread familiarity with online surveys, we asked all employees who belonged to Local 751 of the International Association of Machinists and Aerospace Workers (IAM) and Society of Professional Engineering Employees in Aerospace (SPEEA) unions to participate[2] and gave them the opportunity, if desired, to talk to us. Of those who were willing to be interviewed, we contacted employees who had been employed by the company fewer than five years, endeavoring as before to include men and women who represented the variety of white- and blue-collar jobs at the company. It is from these "new hire" interviews that we chose the narratives to include in part III.

In all, we conducted more than eighty-five interviews between the summer of 2011 and spring of 2014, often over the phone but occasionally in person. The interviews lasted between one and two hours. Although we worked from a list of predetermined questions, we allowed a great deal of latitude during the conversation, both in terms of what employees told us and the scope of our follow-up questions, as we sought to document and understand the richness of each person's experience.[3] We began by asking about their work histories and career progressions, but then moved to questions about coworkers and supervisors, recognition and disappointments, company culture and commitment, expectations and aspirations, and the meaning and significance of their work. We asked them to consider if and how these things had changed over time and, in so doing, captured for many how they saw their work in light of Boeing's changed workplace ethos and, more broadly, the current economic environment and business strategies Boeing and US companies have adopted in recent years.

All the interviews included in the book were taped and transcribed with the permission of the interviewees. The vast majority agreed to publication on condition of anonymity. We have therefore done our best to disguise their identities and, for consistency, have done the same for the few who did not ask for anonymity. The transcripts varied in the length, flow, and thematic structure of their content. In editing them we therefore tried to eliminate repetition and to find the sequential and thematic coherence that they contained. As sociologist Bob Blauner so perceptively points out, editing often involves conflicting goals—seeking to render the stories "economical, clear, and interesting . . . to the reader" while also ensuring they remain "faithful to the original interview."[4] This is what we have assiduously tried to do. To ensure that our editing did not violate the accuracy and spirit of their interviews, we provided the included narratives to thirty-three of the thirty-six employees for any comments they wished to make.[5] While thirty-six in-depth selected interviews cannot be viewed as necessarily representative of the whole Boeing workforce, we are confident that the themes and sentiments expressed in the stories are both salient and ubiquitous. They are themes that employees repeatedly raised in interviews and are consonant with the survey data, summarized in the section introductions.

NOTES

1. BOEING'S TRANSFORMATION AND AMERICA'S NEW SOCIAL CONTRACT

1. In truth, the entirety of Boeing's paradigmatic corporate shift cannot be pinned neatly or solely on the merger. Responding to economic pressures, thousands of Boeing managers had already received trainings on competitiveness in 1994 and 1995, and hundreds of employees, from frontline employees to top executives, toured Toyota's plants in Japan in order to witness world-class efficient production firsthand. Though it took years to fully implement, a new and massive system for managing tens of thousands of parts more cost-efficiently was launched in 1993, and a host of lean manufacturing practices were initiated during this time period. It was, however, the merger with McDonnell Douglas that came to symbolize Boeing's new organizational culture. An extensive description of the merger's effects on employees may be found in Edward Greenberg, Leon Grunberg, Sarah Moore, and Pat Sikora, *Turbulence: Boeing and the State of American Workers and Managers* (New Haven, CT: Yale University Press, 2010).

2. Jeff Cole, "Boeing's Cultural Revolution—Shaken Giant Surrenders Big Dreams for the Bottom Line," *Seattle Times*, December 13, 1998, http://community.seattletimes.nwsource.com/archive/?date=19981213&slug=2788785 (accessed August 12, 2014).

3. This idealized picture of Boeing, while widely endorsed by long-serving employees, was somewhat fueled by nostalgia, regret, and even anger at how Boeing had changed. In reality, worker-management relations, especially with Boeing's blue-collar workforce, had long followed the traditional union-management script. In what might be described as a "wary coexistence," the power-

ful union local of the International Association of Machinists and Aerospace Workers (Local 751) would periodically strike the company to protect or enhance wages, benefits, and job security. The quiescence of the engineering workforce before the merger may perhaps be taken as an indication that they were content with their situation in the company. This changed after the merger, as members of the Society of Professional Engineering Employees in Aerospace went on the largest white-collar strike in US history in 2000, partly to protest their diminished status in the company. David Kusnet goes into some detail on the background and motives for the forty-day strike in *Love the Work, Hate the Job: Why America's Best Workers Are More Unhappy Than Ever* (Hoboken, NJ: Wiley, 2008).

4.   Good overviews of the pressures to change can be found in Christopher Muellerleile, "Financialization Takes Off at Boeing," *Journal of Economic Geography* 9, no. 5 (September 2009): 663–77, and J. Useem, "Boeing v. Boeing," *Fortune* 142, no. 7 (October 2000): 148.

5.   Luke Timmerman, "Stonecipher's Blueprint Built a Stronger Boeing," *Seattle Times*, March 8, 2005, http://www.seattletimes.com/business/stoneciphers-blueprint-built-a-stronger-boeing (accessed January 9, 2015).

6.   The Boeing Commercial Airplanes division currently produces the single-aisle 737, as well as the twin-aisle 747, 777 (sometimes referred to as the Triple 7 by employees), and 787 (cleverly labeled the Dreamliner by Boeing executives). The 767, a twin-aisle commercial jet, has been converted into a tankard and is now produced for the U.S. Air Force. The vast majority of our study participants are from the Commercial Airplanes division, the key revenue and profit generator in the Boeing Company.

7.   Beth Rubin, *Shifts in the Social Contract: Understanding Change in American Society* (Thousand Oaks, CA: Pine Forge Press, 1996); Thomas Kochan, "Employer-Employee New Social Contracts: Fashioning a New Compact," *Academy of Management Perspectives* 21, no. 2 (May 2007): 13–16.

8.   Richard Sennett, *The Corrosion of Character: The Personal Consequences of Work in the New Capitalism* (New York: W. W. Norton, 1998). In *The Unwinding: An Inner History of the New America* (New York: Farrar, Straus and Giroux, 2013), George Packer, surveying the national landscape, has reported on the human effects of what he calls the "unwinding" of the old structures and institutions that anchored the lives of ordinary Americans.

9.   A particularly well-written example of this genre is Bryce Hoffman's *American Icon: Alan Mulally and the Fight to Save Ford Motor Company* (New York: Crown Business, 2012).

10.   Among the best of the many books that document the effects are Jacob S. Hacker, *The Great Risk Shift: The Assault on American Jobs, Families, Health Care, and Retirement* (New York: Oxford University Press, 2006), and

Stephen Greenhouse, *The Big Squeeze: Tough Times for the American Worker* (New York: Alfred A. Knopf, 2008).

11. Details about the study and research methodology can be found in the appendix. To ensure the anonymity of interviewees, we have changed their names and deleted specific details regarding their personal lives and work histories.

12. As early as 2001, L. J. Hart-Smith, a Boeing engineer, wrote an internal report warning Boeing executives about the dangers of excessive outsourcing. L. J. Hart-Smith, "Out-Sourced Profits: The Cornerstone of Successful Sub-contracting," *Seattle Times*, http://seattletimes.nwsource.com/ABPub/2011/02/04/2014130646.pdf.

13. Studs Terkel, *Working: People Talk about What They Do All Day and How They Feel about What They Do* (New York: Avon Books, 1972).

14. John Bowe, Marisa Bowe, and Sabin Streeter, *Gig: Americans Talk about Their Jobs* (New York: Three Rivers Press, 2000).

15. William Whyte, *The Organizational Man* (New York: Simon and Schuster, 1956).

STILL EMPLOYED AT BOEING

1. Many scholarly articles report small but significant generational differences. See, for example, Nicky Dries, Roland Pepermans, and Evelien DeKerpel, "Exploring Four Generations' Beliefs about Career: Is 'Satisfied' the New 'Successful'?," *Journal of Managerial Psychology* 23 (2008): 907–28; Brenda J. Kowske, Rena Rasch, and Jack Wiley, "Millennials' (Lack of) Attitude Problem: An Empirical Examination of Generational Effects on Work Attitudes," *Journal of Business Psychology* 25 (2010): 265–79.

NEWLY HIRED AT BOEING

1. "The Recession of 2007–2009," Bureau of Labor Statistics Spotlight on Statistics, February 2012, http://www.bls.gov/spotlight/2012/recession (accessed May 9, 2015).

2. See, for example, Jennifer Deal, David Altman, and Steven Rogelberg, "Millennials at Work: What We Know and What We Need to Do (if Anything)," *Journal of Business Psychology* 25 (2010): 191–99; Charles Thompson and Jane Gregory, "Managing Millennials: A Framework for Improving Attraction, Motivation, and Retention," *Psychologist-Manager Journal* 15, no. 4

(2012): 237–46; Jean Twenge, "A Review of the Empirical Evidence on Generational Differences in Work Attitudes," *Journal of Business Psychology* 25 (2010): 201–10.

3. In our 2013 survey, those hired in 2007 or afterward represented the Gen Y (28 percent), Gen X (38 percent), and baby boomer (34 percent) cohorts.

9. A SECOND CAREER

1. In 2010, those fifty-five and older spent an average of 35.5 weeks, compared to 23.3 weeks for sixteen- to twenty-four-year-olds and 30.3 weeks for twenty-five- to fifty-four-year-olds. Emy Sok, "Record Unemployment among Older Workers Does Not Keep Them Out of the Job Market," Bureau of Labor Statistics Issues in Labor Statistics, March 2010, http://www.bls.gov/opub/ils/summary_10_04/older_workers.htm (accessed May 9, 2015).

2. William Wiatrowski, "The Last Private Industry Pension Plans: A Visual Essay," *Monthly Labor Review* (December 2012), http://www.bls.gov/opub/mlr/2012/12/art1full.pdf (accessed May 9, 2015).

12. IMPLICATIONS OF THE NEW SOCIAL CONTRACT

1. George Packer, *The Unwinding: An Inner History of the New America* (New York: Farrar, Straus and Giroux, 2013).

2. Analyses between generational cohorts were statistically controlled for length of time worked at the company. Although stage of life rather than generational differences may explain these findings, it is also true that they are in line with much of what has been reported in the scholarly literature and popular press.

3. Nine of the thirty-six interviewees were women, which roughly approximates the proportion found in the company.

4. Boeing's share price is at close to record highs, nearly tripling from what it was in the late 1990s. Lean manufacturing techniques cut 50 percent of the time to complete the assembly of its mainstay, the 737, in 2005, and Boeing has plans to raise the rate of production to forty-seven a month in 2017 from forty-two currently.

5. Boeing is currently losing money on each 787 airplane it delivers. Boeing uses "program accounting" to spread the billions in deferred production

costs over future deliveries of the 787. This accounting method assumes, first, that costs of production will drop as Boeing "learns" how to produce these airplanes more efficiently and, second, that current orders will not vanish in the future in response to a severe market downturn.

6. The case for human resources practices leading to higher performance is well made in Eileen Applebaum et al., *Manufacturing Advantage: Why High Performance Work Systems Pay Off* (Ithaca, NY: Cornell University Press, 2000). Questions about the validity of the association between human resources practices and performance are raised in David Neumark and Peter Cappelli, "Do 'High Performance' Work Practices Improve Establishment-Level Outcomes?," National Bureau of Economic Research, Working Paper 7374, October 1999, http://www.nber.org/papers/w7374.pdf (accessed May 9, 2015), and Benjamin Schneider et al., "Which Comes First: Employee Attitudes or Organizational Financial and Market Performance?," *Journal of Applied Psychology* 88, no. 5 (October 2003): 836–51. Neumark and Cappelli find no statistical evidence of higher productivity for such practices. They do raise employee compensation but do not harm company competitiveness. Schneider et al. find that the association is reversed, with good corporate performance influencing employee attitudes.

7. In answer to a question on what percentage of the workday Boeing employees worked to their full potential, 21 percent reported it was 50 percent or below and 28 percent that it was 60 percent or below.

8. Chapter 8 of Edward Greenberg et al., *Turbulence: Boeing and the State of American Workers and Managers* (New Haven, CT: Yale University Press, 2010), details several of these attitudinal changes and deleterious health consequences.

9. Membership in unions currently hovers in the 11 to 12 percent range across the labor force (but is only 6.7 percent in the private sector), down from 20.1 percent in 1983, and workplace stoppages involving one thousand or more workers are in the low teens after being in the hundreds from 1947 to the late 1970s. Bureau of Labor Statistics, US Department of Labor, "Economic News Release: Table 1. Work Stoppages Involving 1,000 or More Workers, 1947–2014," http://www.bls.gov/news.release/wkstp.t01.htm (accessed May 21, 2015).

10. Useful discussions about the prospective role of labor unions can be found in Richard B. Freeman, "Do Workers Still Want Unions? More Than Ever," Economic Policy Institute, Briefing Paper 182, February 22, 2007, http://www.epi.org/publication/bp182 (accessed May 9, 2015), and Jake Rosenfeld, *What Unions Can No Longer Do* (Boston: Harvard University Press, 2014).

11. Dominic Gates, "Boeing Secretly Testing New Automation for 777X," *Seattle Times,* August 15, 2013, http://www.seattletimes.com/business/boeing-secretly-testing-new-automation-for-777x (accessed May 9, 2015).

12. Lewis Coser, *Greedy Institutions: Patterns of Undivided Commitment* (New York: Free Press, 1974).

APPENDIX

1. A longitudinal panel study follows the same group of individuals over a period of time, taking repeated measures of their responses to the same set of questions. The advantage of this design is that it not only establishes a baseline against which to measure subsequent changes but it also enables researchers to more persuasively connect changes in responses to organizational changes. Methodological details of this longitudinal study may be found in Edward S. Greenberg, Leon Grunberg, Sarah Moore, and Pat Sikora, "Appendix," in *Turbulence: Boeing and the State of American Workers and Managers* (New Haven, CT: Yale University Press, 2010), 195–206.

2. Answers to specific questions and psychometric information about the survey may be obtained from the authors.

3. For example, interviewees who had not been employed by the company during the merger had no firsthand observations of how the company had changed; rather, they were asked about what they had heard from other workers. In addition, for interviewees who had been participants in early phases of our survey research, we also asked questions to follow up on issues (e.g., their health and well-being) they had mentioned previously.

4. Bob Blauner, "Problems of Editing 'First-Person' Sociology," *Qualitative Sociology* 10, no. 1 (Spring 1987): 52.

5. Unfortunately, we could not reach three of the interviewees as their contact information had changed. Of the others, eight suggested small changes so that their identities would be better disguised, and these changes were made.

INDEX

3M, 4

4 flute, 56

401(k), 123, 124, 128, 158, 162, 180

707, 2; accidents, 15

737, 19, 39, 94, 186n6; redesign, 163, 165; workforce, 105, 121

747, 2, 30, 39, 71, 148, 150, 186n6

747-400, 60

757, 14, 35, 96

767, 14, 17, 39, 96, 186n6; Airplane Safety group, 64; designed in Italy, 51, 52–53; flight management systems, 35

777, 14, 17, 36, 54, 71, 121, 186n6; avionics, 30; design, 21, 62; first flight, 60, 61; smooth production and flight-test program, 74

787 Dreamliner, 3, 14, 16, 22, 43, 186n6; 3.5-year delay, 3, 6, 50, 74, 83–84, 99, 152; business model, 50, 74, 86; company pride damaged, 3, 83, 85, 87, 148; cost overruns, 6, 99, 152, 178; failure to do due diligence of test and trial, 16; flight, 43, 61; losing money on each airplane it delivers, 188n5; outsourcing design and production problems, 6, 27, 36–37, 42, 50, 52–53, 60–61, 66, 89, 175; problem with parts, 26, 125; rollout, 95; second assembly line in South Carolina, 3, 50, 58, 87, 94–95, 98, 121, 174, 180; wing structures, 83, 94, 95, 99, 102, 143,

152; workforce, 105, 125, 136

absenteeism, 46

aerospace: engineer, 61; inspector, 132

Airbus, 43, 91, 92, 112, 121–122; accidents, 64

airplane accidents: 707, 15; Airbus, 64; Boeing, 19, 64; surviving, 167

airplanes. *See* Airbus; airplane series number for Boeing; B-2 bomber; E-3 Sentry

airplane safety, 18, 20, 59

Allwood, Cathy, 163–166

Austin, Walt, 123, 124–128

AutoCAD. *See* automated computer-aided design

automated computer-aided design (AutoCAD), 21

avionics, 33

B-2 bomber, 51, 52

baby boomer employees, 47, 105, 107, 108, 176

Bartlett, Wes, 166–169

Blauner, Bob, 184

Boeing, Bill, 2

Boeing airplanes. *See* airplane series number

Boeing Commercial Airplanes, 30, 133, 146, 168, 186n6